Who Regulates Whom and How? An Overview of U.S. Financial Regulatory Policy for Banking and Securities Markets

Edward V. Murphy
Specialist in Financial Economics

May 28, 2013

Congressional Research Service
7-5700
www.crs.gov
R43087

CRS Report for Congress
Prepared for Members and Committees of Congress

Summary

Financial regulatory policies are of interest to Congress because firms, consumers, and governments fund many of their activities through banks and securities markets. Furthermore, financial instability can damage the broader economy. Financial regulation is intended to protect borrowers and investors that participate in financial markets and mitigate financial instability. This report provides an overview of the regulatory policies of the agencies that oversee banking and securities markets and explains which agencies are responsible for which institutions, activities, and markets. Some agencies regulate particular types of institutions for risky behavior or conflicts of interest, some agencies promulgate rules for certain financial transactions no matter what kind of institution engages in them, and other agencies enforce existing rules for some institutions, but not for others. These regulatory activities are not necessarily mutually exclusive.

Banking

U.S. banking regulation traditionally focuses on prudence. Banks' business decisions are regulated for safety and soundness and adequate capital. In addition, banks are given access to a lender of last resort, and some bank creditors are provided guarantees (deposit insurance). Regulating the risks that banks take is believed to help smooth the credit cycle. The credit cycle refers to periodic booms and busts in lending. Prudential safety and soundness regulation and capital requirements date back to the 1860s when bank credit formed the money supply. The Federal Reserve (Fed) as lender of last resort was created following the Panic of 1907. Deposit insurance was established in the 1930s to reduce the incentive of depositors to withdraw funds from banks during a financial panic.

Securities, Derivatives, and Similar Contract Markets

Federal securities regulation has traditionally focused on disclosure and conflicts of interest, rather than on prudence. Securities regulation is typically designed to ensure that market participants have access to enough information to make informed decisions, rather than to limit the riskiness of the business models of publicly traded firms. Firms that sell securities to the public must register with the Securities and Exchange Commission (SEC). SEC registration in no way implies that an investment is safe, only that material risks have been disclosed. The SEC also registers several classes of securities market participants and firms. It has enforcement powers for certain types of industry misstatements or omissions and for certain types of conflicts of interest. Derivatives trading is supervised by the Commodity Futures Trading Commission (CFTC), which oversees trading on the futures exchanges, which have self-regulatory responsibilities as well. The Wall Street Reform and Consumer Protection Act (Dodd-Frank Act, P.L. 111-203) required more disclosures in the over-the-counter (off-exchange) derivatives market than prior to the financial crisis and has granted the CFTC and SEC authority over large derivatives traders.

Government Sponsored Enterprises

The Federal Housing Finance Agency (FHFA) oversees a group of government-sponsored enterprises (GSEs). Two of the GSEs, Fannie Mae and Freddie Mac, securitize residential mortgages, and they were placed in conservatorship following mortgage losses in 2008. In the conservatorship, the Treasury provides financial support to the GSEs and FHFA and Treasury have managerial control over the enterprises. FHFA also regulates the Federal Home Loan Bank

(FHLB) system, a GSE composed of 12 regional banks owned by the 8,000 financial institutions that they serve.

Changes Following the 2008 Financial Crisis

The Dodd-Frank Act created the interagency Financial Stability Oversight Council (FSOC) and authorized a permanent staff to monitor systemic risk and consolidated bank regulation from five agencies to four. The DFA granted the Federal Reserve oversight authority and the Federal Deposit Insurance Corporation (FDIC) resolution authority over the largest financial firms. The Dodd-Frank Act consolidated consumer protection rulemaking, which had been dispersed among several federal agencies, in the new Consumer Financial Protection Bureau.

Special Topics

The appendices in this report include additional information on topics, such as the regulatory structure prior to the Dodd-Frank Act (DFA), organizational differences among financial firms, and the rating system that regulators use to evaluate the health of banks. A list of common acronyms and a glossary of common financial terms are also included as appendices.

Contents

Introduction 1
Policy Problems in Banking and Securities Markets 5
    Banks 5
    Markets to Trade Securities, Futures, and Other Contracts 7
    The Shadow Banking System 9
What Financial Regulators Do 9
    Regulatory Architecture and Categories of Regulation 10
Regulating Banks, Thrifts, and Credit Unions 15
    Safety and Soundness 16
    Capital Requirements 17
    Asset Management 19
    Consumer Protection Compliance 20
    Regulators of Firms with Bank Charters 20
        Office of the Comptroller of the Currency 21
        Federal Deposit Insurance Corporation 21
        The Federal Reserve 23
        National Credit Union Administration 23
Regulating Securities, Derivatives, and Other Contract Markets 23
    Non-Bank Financial Regulators 24
        Securities and Exchange Commission 24
        Commodity Futures Trading Commission 26
        Federal Housing Finance Agency 27
        Consumer Financial Protection Bureau 28
    Regulatory Umbrella Groups 28
        Financial Stability Oversight Council 28
        Federal Financial Institution Examinations Council 29
        President's Working Group on Financial Markets 30
    Non-Bank Capital Requirements 30
        Federal Housing Finance Agency 30
        The SEC's Net Capital Rule 31
        CFTC Capital Requirements 32
    Foreign Exchange Markets 32
    U.S. Treasury Securities 33
    Private Securities Markets 34

Figures

Figure 1. An Example of Regulation of JPMorgan Derivatives Trades 3
Figure B-1. National Bank 37
Figure B-2. National Bank and Subsidiaries 37
Figure B-3. Bank Holding Company 38
Figure B-4. Financial Holding Company 38

Tables

Table 1. Federal Financial Regulators and Organizations 2
Table 2. Policies for Banking Regulation and Securities Regulation 4
Table 3. Federal Financial Regulators and Who They Supervise 13
Table A-1. Capital Standards for Federally Regulated Depository Institutions 36

Appendixes

Appendix A. Capital Requirements: Provisions in Dodd-Frank 35
Appendix B. Forms of Banking Organizations 37
Appendix C. Bank Ratings: UFIRS and CAMELS 39
Appendix D. Regulatory Structure Before the Dodd-Frank Act 41
Appendix D: Acronyms 42
Appendix E. Glossary of Terms 43

Contacts

Author Contact Information 51
Acknowledgments 51

Introduction

Most people in the United States (and other developed nations) have rejected the Shakespearean maxim, "neither a borrower nor a lender be." Many people use loans to finance at least part of their education and job training during their youth, use mortgages to finance at least part of their home while starting a family, invest in stocks and bonds during middle age, and rely on the returns to the value of their stocks, bonds, and homes to at least partially pay for retirement during old age. Business firms, municipalities, and sovereign governments also rely on the financial system to help build the productive capital necessary for a well-functioning society and to foster economic growth. Financial regulatory policies are of interest to Congress because of the repercussions for individual constituents, the financing of firms and governments, and long-run economic growth.

This report provides a framework to help answer the question, "who regulates whom in U.S. financial markets, and how?" At the federal level, the answer often depends on first identifying both the policy problem and the proposed solution. For example, there are federal regulatory overlaps in which one agency can oversee a firm because of the firm's charter, a second agency regulates some of the activities that the firm is engaging in, but a third agency controls a government initiative to resolve or alleviate a problem related to the firm or its activities. On the other hand, there are regulatory gaps in which some of the firms participating in a financial activity do not have regulated charters, and the activity believed to be causing a problem does not have a regulator. Thus, answering "who regulates whom" requires first identifying the problem to be regulated, and how.

This report provides an analysis of financial regulatory policy. It is not intended as a roadmap of legal jurisdiction; rather, it helps to match financial regulatory agencies to financial regulatory policies based on the kinds of financial difficulties that they generally address. Many of these difficulties are related to what economists call *market failures*, which can be loosely described as instances in which market prices and participants do not fully take into account all of the costs and benefits of their actions.

Table 1 presents a list of financial regulators. In the United States, it may be useful to distinguish between regulators that generally focus on *prudence* (i.e., monitoring and regulating the risks that a specific firm engages in) and regulators that generally focus on *disclosure* (i.e., monitoring and regulating the information that firms and exchanges provide to potential market participants). Four federal agencies have prudential authority to examine banks, thrifts, and credit unions.[1] Two agencies oversee markets for financial contracts (securities and derivatives). The agencies listed in the "other" category regulate housing government-sponsored enterprises (GSEs) and consumer financial products, respectively. The entities listed in the coordinating forum category are made up of the other financial regulators with related duties or functions and facilitate communication and coordination among member agencies. Two agencies either regulate an activity regardless of the type of institution that engages in it or provide prudential regulation to nonbanks.[2] The agencies are discussed in more detail below.

---

[1] A fifth agency, the Office of Thrift Supervision (OTS), was abolished in 2010, and its responsibilities were spread among other agencies. Its prudential regulation of thrift depositories was transferred to the Office of the Comptroller of the Currency. Its prudential regulation of thrift holding companies was transferred to the Federal Reserve.

[2] The Federal Reserve also provides prudential regulation to certain nonbank financial companies and financial-market (continued...)

Table 1. Federal Financial Regulators and Organizations
(acronyms and area of authority)

Prudential Bank Regulators	Securities and Derivatives Regulators	Other Regulators of Financial Activities	Coordinating Forum
Office of the Comptroller of the Currency (OCC)	Securities and Exchange Commission (SEC)	Federal Housing Finance Agency (FHFA)	Financial Stability Oversight Council (FSOC)
Federal Deposit Insurance Corporation (FDIC)	Commodities Futures Trading Commission (CFTC)	Consumer Financial Protection Bureau (CFPB)	Federal Financial Institutions Examinations Council (FFIEC)
National Credit Union Administration (NCUA)			President's Working Group on Capital Markets (PWG)
Federal Reserve Board (FRB, or the Fed)			

Source: The Congressional Research Service (CRS).

The policy problems and regulatory approaches of the agencies listed in **Table 1** vary considerably. Before providing a detailed analysis of each agency, it may be useful to consider how the agencies are related to each other and briefly sketch the types of policies they generally pursue. The prudential bank regulators and the Federal Housing Finance Agency (FHFA) examine firms with specific charters and monitor and limit the risks that their chartered firms engage in. Securities and derivatives regulators monitor exchanges that host the trading of financial contracts, oversee the disclosures that market participants provide, and enforce rules against deceptive or manipulative trading practices. Unlike prudential bank regulators, securities regulators generally do not monitor the composition of assets and liabilities of the firms participating in their markets (although they may require collateral or margin to be posted for some activities, and they may monitor the financial condition of exchanges).[3] These and other general differences may exist because of the various missions and risks to financial stability that the agencies address.

A specific event in the financial industry is often regulated by multiple agencies because firms subject to institution-based regulation often conduct financial transactions that that are subject to activity-based regulation. JPMorgan's losses in derivatives markets in 2012 may provide a helpful illustration. JPMorgan's depository bank subsidiary had a risk management unit called CIO. This unit had significant losses on trades related to complex derivatives (called the London Whale trades at the time), which JPMorgan asserted were designed to guard against systemic risk. When revelations of the losses became public, and people wanted to know who JPMorgan's regulator was, the answer was that there were many regulators related to JPMorgan's London Whale trades, depending upon which aspect of the event a person was interested in.

(...continued)
utilities that are designated as systemic.

[3] Although the distinction between prudence-based regulators and disclosure-based regulators may be true in general, bank regulators can regulate the disclosures of their chartered firms and securities and derivatives regulators do have some prudential responsibilities. For example, Section 731 of the Dodd-Frank Act instructs derivatives regulators to set capital requirements for major swap participants.

The regulatory policy areas of agencies related to JPMorgan's derivatives trades are presented in **Figure 1**. As a bank, JPMorgan's risk management was subject to prudential regulation by the OCC at the depository level, and by the Federal Reserve on a consolidated basis at the holding company level. As a public company, JPMorgan's disclosures of the trades to its stockholders were regulated by the SEC. As a participant in derivatives markets, JPMorgan's transactions were subject to CFTC regulation. As an insured depository institution, JPMorgan's safety and soundness was also subject to the FDIC.

Figure 1. An Example of Regulation of JPMorgan Derivatives Trades

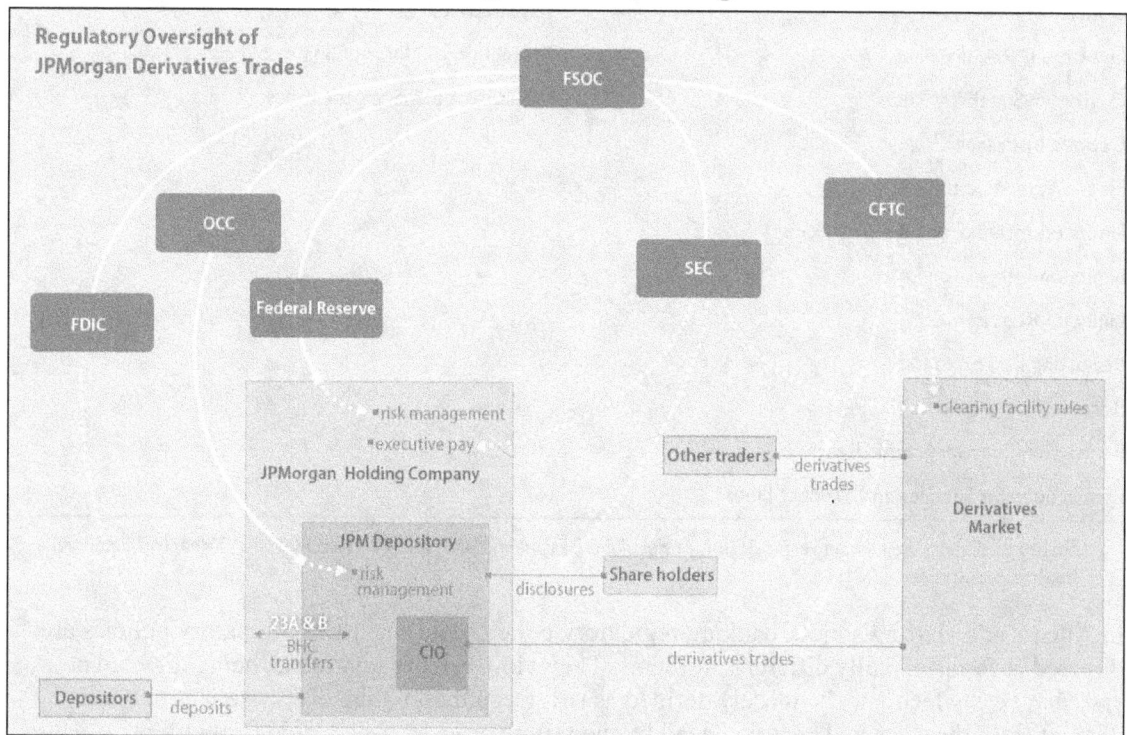

Source: CRS.

Table 2 compares the general policy options and approaches of the banking regulators to the securities market regulators, which is drawn from *Banking Regulation versus Securities Regulation*, by Franklin Allen and Richard Herring. The table lists many of the categories of regulations that are often considered for banks and securities markets. It does not mean that each category is in place at all times; for example, there have been times during which the United States has restricted interest payments on bank deposits, and times when the United States has not. Many of these categories of policy options are discussed in more detail in later sections of this report.

Table 2. Policies for Banking Regulation and Securities Regulation

Types of Banking Regulatory Policies	Types of Securities Regulatory Policies
Asset Restrictions	Disclosure Standards
Capital Adequacy	Registration Requirements
Conduct of Business Rules	Manipulation Prohibition
Competition Policy (Anti-Trust)	Insider Trading Prohibition
Conflict of Interest Rules	Takeover Rules
Investment Requirements	Protection of Minority Shareholders
Customer Suitability Rules	Investment Management Rules
Deposit Insurance	
Fit and Proper Entry Tests	
Limits on Interest on Deposits	
Limits on Interest on Loans	
Liquidity Requirements	
Reporting Large Transactions	
Reserve Requirements	
Restrictions on Geographic Reach	
Restrictions on Services and Product Lines	

Source: *Banking Regulation versus Securities Regulation*, Franklin Allen and Richard Herring, Wharton Financial Institutions Center, 2001.

In Allen's and Herring's view, banking regulatory policies and securities regulatory policies are directed at fundamentally different problems. They view bank regulation as being directed at *systemic risk*, which may be loosely defined as risk faced by the financial system as a whole, distinct from the costs and benefits faced by the failure or losses of a single firm or a price movement in a single market. In contrast, they attribute many of the securities market regulator's policies to *investor protection* and *efficiency enhancement* (including aligning corporate management with stockholder interests). Therefore, it may be useful to compare the general policy problems of banking and securities markets.

This report is organized as follows. The first section briefly discusses several policy problems associated with financial intermediation. The second section describes various modes of financial regulation to address these concerns and includes a table identifying the major federal regulators and the types of institutions and markets they supervise. The table also identifies certain emergency authorities available to the regulators, including those that relate to systemic financial disturbances. The third section focuses on the regulation of firms with bank charters. The fourth section focuses on the regulation of financial trading markets, especially securities and derivatives. The fifth section focuses on certain other financial regulators and markets that either do not easily fit into banking or securities or markets that do not have a dedicated regulator. The appendices topics include organizational differences among financial firms, the rating system that regulators use to evaluate the health of banks, the regulatory structure prior to the Dodd-Frank Act, a list of common acronyms, and a glossary of common financial terms.

Policy Problems in Banking and Securities Markets

Ultimately, the function of the financial system is to coordinate the flow of resources from savers to borrowers, and back again. Two common methods to provide this financial intermediation include (1) firms that directly gather funds from savers to directly lend to borrowers (banks, for example) and (2) markets that facilitate the trading of financial obligations (securities and derivatives exchanges, for example). The range of financial obligations includes, but is not limited to,

- debts—repayment of principal and interest,
- equities—share in ownership and returns,
- hybrids—mixture of debt and equity features,
- insurance—payment contingent on occurrence of a future event,
- swaps—promises to exchange one type of stream of payment for another, and
- forwards—promises for future delivery at a particular place and time.

Although there are many ways to organize a firm that offers bank-like services, and there are many types of contracts that combine elements of bank-like loans with securities contracts, the regulation of the financial system in the United States has historically focused on distinguishing banks, securities markets, and insurance.

The analytical tradition in the United States has been to distinguish commercial banking from investment banking. Commercial banks accept customer deposits and offer commercial loans. Investment banks underwrite and register new securities and market them to individual or institutional investors. Investment banks also provide brokerage services, advice on corporate financing and proprietary trading, and assistance to merger and acquisition proposals.

Although insurance issues are beyond the scope of this report, banking and securities markets are discussed briefly below.

Banks

Banks are intermediaries between savers and borrowers. In its simplest form, the business model of commercial banks is to accept deposits from savers in order to make loans to borrowers—in other words, banks borrow from depositors and offer loans to individuals, business firms, nonprofits, and governments. Although savers could offer loans directly to potential borrowers, there are several advantages of relying on specialized lenders. For example, savers essentially pay banks to act on their behalf (an agency relationship[4]), identifying credit-worthy borrowers, writing and administering loan contracts, and enforcing the loan terms if the borrower defaults. Another potential source of profit centers on timing. Since long-term interest rates are generally higher than short-term interest rates, banks can earn profits by borrowing short-term in order to offer longer-term loans (often referred to as a maturity transformation or maturity mismatch).

---

[4] The term *agency* is being used to describe the functional relationship and does not imply any contractual obligation.

This is not an exhaustive list of commercial bank services or earnings, but it is a useful list to illustrate several recurring economic issues.

The business model of banks also creates a number of economic policy problems. Like any other agency relationship, bank managers do not necessarily always act in the best interests of bank investors or depositors. The maturity mismatch makes banks vulnerable to interest rate volatility and to "runs" if depositors withdraw their funds simultaneously in a panic. The effort to identify credit-worthy borrowers and projects can cause bankers to affect pools of borrowers in ways that create credit shortages, or base lending decisions on criteria that do not further social goals of the community (e.g., discrimination).

These policy problems may be addressed by regulations for individual banks. Some of these regulations include restrictions on conflicts of interest of bank managers, the use of deposits, and the ability of depositors to withdraw their funds; limitations on the proportion of bank resources that can be devoted to or drawn from particular markets or counterparties; rules on the loan application process; and laws to prevent lending discrimination.

Banking is also subject to systemic problems beyond the activities of any one institution. Another potential source of profit (related to the agency relationship) is for the bank to take excessive risk. That is, compared with other banks, an individual bank can keep fewer resources available against the possibility of depositor withdrawal, or offer more loans in the heightened-risk categories (that typically pay higher interest), and depend on its ability to borrow from other banks if it suffers excessive withdrawals or higher defaults. Although a single bank that follows a higher-risk strategy might be able to borrow from other banks if it suffers higher than expected losses or greater than expected depositor withdrawals, all banks cannot successfully follow this strategy simultaneously because there would be too few healthy banks to borrow from should loan defaults be higher than expected or should depositors withdraw funds in greater amounts than expected.

This systemic banking problem involves a fallacy of composition, and it can be illustrated using the example of a stadium. If a single person stands at the stadium, it is likely that the person will be able to see the event better, but if everyone stands in the stadium, most people will not have a better view of the event and will be less comfortable. Similarly, if a single bank expands its lending for a given amount of capital, that bank is likely to make higher profits without endangering financial stability, but if many banks follow a similar strategy, none gains a competitive advantage over the others, and all are less able to obtain interbank loans during a crisis.

Excessive risk taking by banks can have systemic consequences. One systemic problem may be that a large number of banks will attempt to borrow from each other at the same time, causing a spike in interest rates or the absence of new bank credit altogether. If many banks follow this strategy, then all banks may be unable to find an institution willing and able to lend to them in the event of depositor withdrawals, and the banking system as a whole may temporarily cease to be a source of credit for the wider economy.

Banks might contribute to a boom-bust cycle for debt-sensitive assets. During booms, banks that intend to rely on emergency lending from other banks may offer too much credit, and on terms that do not adequately account for the risk that the bank's own access to credit may decline if market conditions change. The resulting cheap credit may help fuel a price bubble in the asset or trading activity financed with the debt. During busts, more banks are likely to fail than would have occurred if banks had reserved the appropriate amount of resources for the amount of risk that they incurred. Thus, the higher bank failure rate (compared to if more banks had been cautious during the boom) could cause the total amount of credit available to the wider economy to shrink more than would have occurred if financial risks had been adequately accounted for.

There are a number of possible policy responses to these systemic concerns in banking. Bank regulators can be empowered to restrict bank balance sheets. Some of these restrictions, discussed in more detail below, include safety and soundness regulation and requirements to hold adequate capital. Even though these regulations may be applied at the institution level, they have systemic effects because in the aggregate the lending activity of the banking system as a whole has an important impact on credit booms and busts. Bank depositors could be offered insurance to reduce their incentive to withdraw funds. Banks that cannot borrow from other banks during emergencies can be provided a lender of last resort.

Markets to Trade Securities, Futures, and Other Contracts

In contrast to a commercial banking institution that originates and holds loans, a securities market is just a venue to exchange financial contracts. Markets can facilitate the trading of debts, equities, futures, or a variety of other financial instruments. Financial institutions that help facilitate the marketing of debts, equities and other financial instruments are sometimes called investment banks.

Although these financial markets are being presented as an alternative to commercial banking, there is no reason that a commercial bank would be unable to participate in securities markets as either a buyer or a seller (although in some cases it may be unlawful to do so). Loans to the government of the United States may be a useful illustration. While it is possible for a single bank to originate and hold an individual loan to the U.S. government, the borrowing of the government is overwhelmingly conducted by issuing debts (Treasury securities) that are traded. Banks are just one group among the many buyers of U.S. Treasury securities. Private firms have also issued tradable debt securities for centuries. Like lending institutions, tradable contracts have a long history and are subject to a number of well-known potential market failures.

Several enduring economic inefficiencies related to securities markets are caused by the limited availability of information and potential conflicts of interest. Some market participants may have an information advantage—such as providers of confidential services to financial firms. A related issue is the "lemons problem," named for the used-car market in which potential buyers of used cars might discount all used cars because of the fear that used-car salesmen may withhold negative information about the quality of a specific car being offered. Potential securities buyers may fall prey to securities dealers and brokers if the latter have an incentive to help place securities that the seller knows may have some undisclosed flaw (lemons). Furthermore, like any agent[5] relationship, securities professionals may not always act in the best interests of their clients.

Other potential economic inefficiencies can arise that are related to specific types of contracts that are traded. For example, some financial contracts are for future delivery of a physical commodity, such as wheat of a certain quality and quantity, at a particular place and time (forward or futures

---

[5] The term *agent* is being used to describe the functional relationship, not any contractual obligations.

contract). This means that at any time, for example, there will be both a spot market for wheat (its price to be obtained currently) and the forward price (the current price for delivery on the specified future date). If there is no formal organization of trading rules, it might be possible for someone to use forward contracts to lock up most of the deliverable supply on a specific future date, leaving only a "corner" of the spot market for sale on that date. But even if such attempts to corner commodity markets are rarely successful, the attempts themselves might introduce additional price distortions that could contribute to financial instability.

Potential economic inefficiencies are also related to formal trading organizations and platforms, if they are used. Having experienced many of the policy problems described above, financial traders have from time to time organized formal market exchanges, adopted rules of trading, and limited membership. However, the exchange itself can then become a potential source of financial instability if it does not have enough resources to withstand the failure of one of its members to honor its obligations to the exchange, or if its rules exacerbate the problems described above. For example, nonmembers of the exchange could lose confidence (and willingness to participate) if they feel that members have important trading advantages, such as if the trades of members are executed first even if they are not submitted first.

There are a number of policy responses to concerns related to trading financial contracts. Some are listed in **Table 2**, including requiring that securities and traders be registered and investors be provided adequate disclosures regarding the characteristics of the securities. Given that formal exchanges are organized in part to address some of the known inefficiencies, policymakers might require that certain types of contracts be traded on formal exchanges. The organization and membership of the formal exchanges could be regulated. Providers of securities-related services may be regulated for minimum professional qualifications and potential conflicts of interest. Issuers of new securities may be required to meet certain financial thresholds and disclose specific information in a format and venue that is readily accessible to the investing public. Some potential buyers of securities may be excluded for lack of sufficient financial literacy or sophistication or have to exceed a minimum financial wherewithal (as a proxy or substitute for sophistication).

Securities markets may also create systemic concerns. Like bank lending, if securities markets fail to adequately address the risks of the activities being funded (thus overstating potential rewards compared with risks), then "too much" savings may be channeled into a particular asset class. As a result, prices in that asset class will tend to be bid up until the true risks manifest themselves, at which time the market collapses. Leveraged and collateralized funding can also cause securities markets to contribute to a boom-bust cycle. That is, if securities buyers are able to increase their purchasing power with debt, especially if the purchased securities form the collateral of the loan, then a decline in the price of the security can lead to "fire sales" as the loans taken out by the buyers default, and then the securities purchased with the loans are liquidated in an already falling market. Some are concerned that algorithmic or program trading can also contribute to systemic events if unanticipated events or technical shortcomings cause trading algorithms, which may be on autopilot, to pursue extreme strategies.

A number of possible policies can address systemic concerns in securities markets. One approach is to temporarily halt trading if market prices vary by more than some pre-specified amount during a set time. Another approach is to limit the amount, and collateral, of debt that can be used to fund securities purchases under some circumstances. Yet another approach is to require firms that facilitate securities issuance to retain some of the risk of the securities issued, sometimes referred to as *skin in the game*.

The Shadow Banking System

As discussed above, banking and securities markets are not mutually exclusive, nor are all financial obligations easily categorized. The term *shadow banking* is sometimes used to refer to the funding of loans through securities markets instead of banks—or to the funding of banks through securities markets instead of deposits. Other times, shadow banking is used to refer to financial activity that is ineligible for a government backstop. One type of government backstop is a financial guarantee, such as deposit insurance. Another type is access to emergency loans from the government, such as the ability to borrow from the Federal Reserve's discount window. What the definitions have in common is they describe alternatives to the simplistic banking model, that is, alternatives to banks that are funded with insured deposits and that only offer commercial loans.

Parts of the shadow banking system are regulated. For example, a lender could borrow money through securities markets rather than from traditional retail depositors. One way to do that is through a repurchase agreement (repo), in which the lender sells a security (such as a U.S. Treasury) today and promises to repurchase it in the near future at a higher price. The price differential represents a form of interest payment similar to a collateralized loan. Thus, rather than a bank borrowing money from traditional depositors, a bank can borrow from other financial institutions through repos. If a chartered bank signs a repo with a chartered bank, both firms are banks and both are regulated; nevertheless, under some definitions the transaction would be considered shadow banking. However, chartered banks are not the only firms that can use repurchase agreements—non-banks can raise funds through repurchase agreements in order to fund other investments, including loans. If a non-bank signs a repo with a non-bank, and uses the proceeds to fund other investments, neither non-bank may be subject to prudential regulation, have access to the Federal Reserve's discount window, have creditors with deposit insurance.

The repos described above are only one of many alternatives to deposits that can be used to fund loans. Other examples include relatively short-term commercial debt that is backed by pools of loans (asset-backed commercial paper, or ABCP). A bank could sponsor a facility that issues ABCP in order to buy loans. If so, the bank's participation (usually promising to provide liquidity if the market is unexpectedly disrupted) is subject to prudential regulation. As with repos, banks are not the only firms that can sponsor ABCP; thus, it is possible for the market to be funded by firms without access to the Fed's discount window and without insured deposits. However, activities being called shadow banking are often still subject to securities regulation.

Many of the general policy problems of banks and securities markets also apply to shadow banking. For example, if a class of loans (such as mortgages or sovereign debt) is funded through securities markets, potential flaws in securities issuance and pricing can contribute to a boom-bust cycle in assets purchased with those loans. If nonbanks (such as money market mutual funds and hedge funds) invest a fraction of the funds they gather, and promise to allow their own investors to withdraw funds at will, these nonbanks can suffer runs if many investors attempt to withdraw simultaneously. The reach of financial regulators to address policy problems in shadow banking varies from activity to activity and from class of firm to class of firm.

What Financial Regulators Do

The regulatory missions of individual agencies vary, sometimes as a result of historical accident. Some agencies have powers over particular firms, but not over all of the other participants in the market that the firm might participate in. Other regulators have authority over markets or activities, and this authority applies to a variety of the firms that participate. As a result, a single firm might have to answer to both the regulator of its charter and to the regulator of a particular activity (i.e., regulatory overlap). However, there may also be instances in which a corner of the financial system has neither a regulator of the specific firms, nor a regulator of the particular activities (i.e., regulatory gap). This section of the report summarizes several categories of regulation, provides a table of specific financial regulators in the United States and their policy spheres, and describes the basic regulatory approach for banks (prudence) and securities markets (disclosure).

Regulatory Architecture and Categories of Regulation

The term *regulatory architecture* describes the organization of the agencies that regulate a particular policy sphere. A possible architecture is to have a single regulatory agency with examination powers over all industry firms, rulemaking authority for all industry-related activities, and power to enforce its rules and resolve controversies that arise in the industry. An alternative architecture is to have specialized regulators that focus on a subset of industry-related policy problems.

The United States has historically provided one or more regulator for each category of financial regulation, rather than a single agency with authority for all financial markets, activities, and institutions. From time to time, the perceived drawbacks to the multiplicity of federal regulators bring forth calls for regulatory consolidation. Even prior to the financial panic in September 2008, the Department of the Treasury had issued a framework for financial reform.[6] After the crisis, the legislative debate over the Dodd-Frank Act included different views on the topic: early versions of the Senate bill would have replaced all the existing bank regulators with a single Financial Institution Regulatory Authority. Dodd-Frank created two new agencies (and numerous regulatory offices) and merged the Office of Thrift Supervision (OTS) with the Office of the Comptroller of the Currency (OCC).

Choosing a regulatory architecture may involve trade-offs. As one economist explained,

> On the one hand, one might conclude that the need to compete with other agencies would motivate a regulator to perform its tasks as effectively and efficiently as possible. On the other hand, one might argue that the desire to attract more clients could drive a regulatory agency to be loose.[7]

In addition, it is not clear that countries with single regulators fare better during crises or are more successful at preventing them. For example, the 2008 financial crisis damaged the financial systems of countries with significantly different regulatory approaches. While the U.S. response was to create a single council to coordinate its varied regulators, the United Kingdom (UK) in May 2010 broke up its Financial Services Authority, which had jurisdiction over securities, banking, derivatives, and insurance.

---

[6] See, e.g., U.S. Department of the Treasury, *Blueprint for a Modern Financial Regulatory Structure*, March 2008, which called for a three-agency structure: a systemic risk regulator, a markets supervisor, and a consumer regulator.

[7] "Competition Among Bank Regulators," John Weinberg, *Economic Quarterly*, Fall 2002, available at http://www.richmondfed.org/publications/research/economic_quarterly/2002/fall/pdf/weinberg.pdf.

Here is a description of different ways to regulate financial firms and services:

- **Regulate Certain Types of Financial Institutions.** Some firms become subject to federal regulation when they obtain a particular business charter, and several federal agencies regulate only a single class of institution. Depository institutions are a good example: a depository may be subject to the regulations of multiple prudential regulators, but typically only one agency is granted primary oversight authority based on the bank's charter—national bank, state bank, credit union, etc.—and the choice of charter may not greatly affect the institution's permissible business mix. Government-sponsored enterprises (GSEs) also have a primary prudential regulator.

  Regulation keyed to particular institutions has at least two perceived disadvantages. First, regulator shopping, or *regulatory arbitrage*, may occur if regulated entities can choose their regulator. Second, unchartered firms engaging in the identical business activity as regulated firms may escape institutional regulation altogether.

- **Regulate a Particular Market.** Some markets become subject to federal financial regulation when they host the trading of covered financial products. The New York Stock Exchange (NYSE) and the Chicago Mercantile Exchange (CME) are two examples. The Securities and Exchange Commission (SEC) regulates the trading of stocks and bonds and the Commodity Futures Trading Commission (CFTC) regulates the trading of commodity futures. The SEC and CFTC generally do not regulate the prices of stocks or futures traded on the exchanges; rather, they regulate the organization and membership of the exchanges, rules for trading, and attempt to prevent fraud, conflicts of interest, or manipulation by market participants.

  Regulation keyed to markets has at least two perceived disadvantages. First, market evolution can create jurisdictional ambiguities among the regulators. Second, innovation in financial products may create regulatory gaps.

- **Regulate a Particular Financial Activity.** Some financial activities are subject to federal regulation no matter which institutions engage in them and no matter who hosts the trades in them. For example, the Consumer Financial Protection Bureau (CFPB) regulates certain classes of loans to consumers no matter who extends the loan (bank or nonbank). If the lender is a bank, the lender has to comply with both the regulations of the CFPB and the rules of its bank regulator.

  Regulation keyed to activities can be problematic. As discussed above, there are often multiple methods to achieve similar financial objectives (combining different contracts). Therefore, if one type of transaction is regulated, it may be possible for people to use another type of contract, one that is not currently regulated or through institutions that are not regulated.

- **Regulate for Systemic Risk.** One definition of systemic risk is that it occurs when each firm manages risk rationally from its own perspective, but the sum total of those decisions produces systemic instability under certain conditions. Similarly, regulators charged with overseeing individual parts of the financial system may satisfy themselves that no threats to stability exist in their respective sectors, but fail to detect risks arising from the interaction of firms and markets. Yet, regulation of institutions, markets, and activities may also have a component of systemic risk regulation. For example, regulation of bank capital may affect the potential for booms and busts in asset markets. The Dodd-Frank Act created the Financial Stability Oversight Council (FSOC) to assume a coordinating role among the heads of financial regulatory agencies; the FSOC has a permanent staff to monitor financial-sector risks as a whole.

What does it mean to be regulated?

It is common to refer to a firm or a market as being regulated or unregulated. However, this simplification can mask important distinctions for any given policy discussion because regulators can have limited scope of operation. That is, agencies may have rulemaking authority or enforcement powers to address one set of policy concerns but not for other policy issues. Firms may be subject to different regulators for different aspects of their business.

The point can be illustrated with a more familiar industry. Are restaurants regulated? There is no federal Department of Restaurants; however, the Occupational Safety and Health Administration (OSHA) can make rules for worker safety (including food service employees), and the Department of Justice can enforce employment discrimination laws (including in restaurants). Furthermore, restaurants are typically subject to state and local health inspectors and related laws. If the policy topic is health and safety, it would be inaccurate to characterize restaurants as unregulated. On the other hand, many potential policy issues related to restaurants are typically unregulated. For example, the restaurant menu and prices are not typically regulated. A food service is typically free to pair nonstandard items (white wine with red meat) and charge very high prices.

Are financial institutions, markets, and activities regulated? Like the restaurant example above, the answer depends on the policy issue being discussed. Take the example of stocks. Firms with outstanding common stock must register with the SEC, file a prospectus, and make regular public disclosures. Marketplaces that facilitate stock market trading must register and comply with SEC regulations. However, the price of an individual stock is not typically regulated, and the amount of stock that an individual firm wishes to offer for sale is not typically regulated. However, even stock prices and trading volume may be subject to circuit breakers to temporarily limit trading during periods of exceptional volatility.

The information in **Table 3** sets out the general federal financial regulatory architecture for banks and securities markets. **Appendix D** contains a pre-Dodd-Frank version of the same table. Supplemental material—charts that illustrate the differences between banks, bank holding companies, and financial holding companies—appears in **Appendix B**.

Table 3. Federal Financial Regulators and Who They Supervise

Regulatory Agency	Institutions Regulated	Emergency/Systemic Risk Powers	Other Notable Authority
Federal Reserve	Bank holding companies and certain subsidiaries, financial holding companies, securities holding companies, savings and loan holding companies, and any firm designated as systemically significant by the FSOC. State banks that are members of the Federal Reserve System, U.S. branches of foreign banks, and foreign branches of U.S. banks. Payment, clearing, and settlement systems designated as systemically significant by the FSOC, unless regulated by SEC or CFTC.	Lender of last resort to member banks (through discount window lending) In "unusual and exigent circumstances," the Fed may extend credit beyond member banks, to provide liquidity to the financial system, but not to aid failing financial firms. May initiate resolution process to shut down firms that pose a grave threat to financial stability (requires concurrence of two-thirds of the FSOC). The FDIC and the Treasury Secretary have similar powers.	Numerous market-level regulatory authorities, such as checking services, lending markets, and other banking-related activities.
Office of the Comptroller of the Currency (OCC)	National banks, federally chartered thrift institutions		
Federal Deposit Insurance Corporation (FDIC)	Federally insured depository institutions, including state banks and thrifts that are not members of the Federal Reserve System.	After making a determination of systemic risk, the FDIC may invoke broad authority to use the deposit insurance funds to provide an array of assistance to depository institutions, including debt guarantees.	Operates a deposit insurance fund for federally and state chartered banks and thrifts.
National Credit Union Administration (NCUA)	Federally chartered or insured credit unions	Serves as a liquidity lender to credit unions experiencing liquidity shortfalls through the Central Liquidity Facility.	Operates a deposit insurance fund for credit unions, known as the National Credit Union Share Insurance Fund (NCUSIF).

Regulatory Agency	Institutions Regulated	Emergency/Systemic Risk Powers	Other Notable Authority
Securities and Exchange Commission (SEC)	Securities exchanges, brokers, and dealers; clearing agencies; mutual funds; investment advisers (including hedge funds with assets over $150 million)	May unilaterally close markets or suspend trading strategies for limited periods.	Authorized to set financial accounting standards in which all publicly traded firms must use.
	Nationally recognized statistical rating organizations		
	Security-based swap (SBS) dealers, major SBS participants, and SBS execution facilities		
	Corporations selling securities to the public must register and make financial disclosures.		
Commodity Futures Trading Commission (CFTC)	Futures exchanges, brokers, commodity pool operators, and commodity trading advisors	May suspend trading, order liquidation of positions during market emergencies.	
	Swap dealers, major swap participants, and swap execution facilities		
Federal Housing Finance Agency (FHFA)	Fannie Mae, Freddie Mac, and the Federal Home Loan Banks	Acting as conservator (since Sept. 2008) for Fannie Mae and Freddie Mac	
Bureau of Consumer Financial Protection	Nonbank mortgage-related firms, private student lenders, payday lenders, and larger "consumer financial entities" to be determined by the Bureau		Writes rules to carry out the federal consumer financial protection laws
	Consumer businesses of banks with over $10 billion in assets		
	Does not supervise insurers, SEC and CFTC registrants, auto dealers, sellers of nonfinancial goods, real estate brokers and agents, and banks with assets less than $10 billion		

Source: The Congressional Research Service (CRS), with information drawn from agency websites, and financial regulatory legislation.

a. See **Appendix B**.

Regulating Banks, Thrifts, and Credit Unions

In general, the term *bank* will be used in this section to refer to firms (or subsidiaries) with bank, thrift, or credit union charters.[8] Banking regulators in the United States attempt to address many of the general policy problems described in the introduction by focusing on the health of chartered banks. Bank charters limit the range of permissible activities and affiliations of banks. Bank regulators employ examiners to monitor and evaluate the financial health of the banks they regulate. Furthermore, deposit insurance and a system to coordinate bank reserves and provide emergency lending is available to participating banks. The primary prudential regulator of a given bank depends on its charter; however, other policies (such as lending to a troubled bank or resolving a failed bank) are applied by a single agency regardless of the charter. Activity-based regulation applies to chartered banks—thus the SEC retains its authority for communications between publicly traded banks and their stockholders, and the CFPB regulates many classes of loans that banks make to consumers.

Is this a bank?

Functionally, the simplest form of bank accepts deposits in order to offer loans.[9] Although this is not a legal definition of a bank, it does capture the basic intermediary function of banking. In practice, it is often difficult to precisely distinguish banking from other services. It is tempting to ascribe this difficulty to financial innovation, but in reality many modern "innovations" are really just minor variations on old practices. Because in discussions of financial regulation, the term *bank* is often reserved for firms with specific charters, it may be useful to distinguish chartered-depository banks from other institutions and people who offer similar services.

Many institutions and organizations have offered bank-like services throughout history. For example, ancient Chinese records describe lenders that required borrowers to offer small goods as collateral for loans (similar to a modern pawn shop). People in Medieval Europe sometimes deposited precious metals with silversmiths (who had their own reasons for extra security) for safekeeping, and some silversmiths then offered loans to third parties, counting on the depositors to not withdraw simultaneously.

One controversial example is Whalebone Cafe Bank (WCB), an ice cream shop in Pittsburgh, Pennsylvania. Reportedly, customers can make a deposit at the ice cream shop and receive the equivalent of 5.5% interest in gift cards for ice cream and other goods sold at the store.[10] It has also been reported that WCB offered loans, including a $510-cash loan to a man who will pay it back in $60 installments, which includes a $25 fee. The Pennsylvania Department of Banking, according to reports, is investigating, but there are questions as to whether the agency can shut down an ice cream shop or ban stores from rewarding customers with gift cards.[11]

Several major banking laws limit their application to firms with federally insured deposits, specific banking charters, or affiliations with depository banks. As a result, some investment firms that are sometimes referred to as Wall Street banks are not banks for certain regulatory purposes, nor are some pawn shops and ice cream stores, even if they offer bank-like services.

---

[8] Illustrations of several forms of depository organization are presented in **Appendix B**.

[9] Historically, "banks" also referred to firms with special charters that issued debt, which often circulated as currency. The Bank of England had been granted a monopoly on this form of banking (note issue), which was determined not to extend to depository banking in the nineteenth century.

[10] As described in a *Wall Street Journal* article, available at http://online.wsj.com/article/ SB10000872396390444433504577649971326432962.html.

[11] This report will not track the ultimate fate of the ice cream shop. The owner reportedly changed the name to remove the word bank. Regulatory interaction is likely to be ongoing. For example, see "Pittsburgh ice cream bank owner says regulators are backing off," WTAE News, available at http://www.wtae.com/news/local/allegheny/Pittsburgh-ice-cream-bank-owner-says-regulators-are-backing-off/-/10927008/19522712/-/asy08i/-/index.html.

As listed in **Table 1**, four prudential regulators coordinate the examinations policies of depositories through the Federal Financial Institution Examinations Council (FFIEC) in order to prevent inconsistencies in the stringency of regulatory oversight. A bank or thrift may organize itself with a depository subsidiary owned by a larger holding company, in which case the holding company may have a different primary regulator than the depository subsidiary. The OCC regulates depository banks and thrifts that have a federal charter (subsidiaries if in a holding company structure). The FDIC regulates banks with a state charter that are not members of the Federal Reserve System (subsidiaries if in a holding company structure). The NCUA regulates credit unions that have a federal charter. In addition to these federal regulators, state governments have their own agencies to administer state banking laws. The Federal Reserve regulates state-chartered member banks (subsidiaries) and holding companies of banks and thrifts. The Conference of State Bank Supervisors (CSBS) serves as a forum for state banking agencies, but is not itself a regulator. State banking supervisors choose a nonvoting representative to serve the FSOC in an advisory capacity.

Many prudential regulations are of degree, not of kind. That is, there are many categories of activities that banks may participate in, but they must either limit their concentration or offset related risks in another manner. For example, banks may offer 30-year fixed-rate mortgages; but, an individual bank may have to manage its resulting interest rate risk by offering other loans with shorter maturities or by acquiring derivatives that hedge interest rate risk. As a result, prudential regulation is not always about catching lawbreakers or policing legal violations, but is often about monitoring the risks that banks engage in or the procedures bank managers have in place to control risk. Even banks that have not violated any statute may be required to adjust their lending or other business practices in response to the regulator's evaluation of risks in current conditions.

This section describes five prominent elements of bank regulation that each primary prudential regulator supervises for its chartered firms: (1) safety and soundness, (2) capital requirements, (3) asset management, (4) consumer compliance, and (5) community reinvestment. In many cases the primary prudential regulator will not be the sole policymaker or regulatory authority for these issues. For example, rules for capital requirements and safety and soundness may be coordinated with other bank regulators, and banks may have to comply with consumer regulations issued by the CFPB in addition to satisfying their own primary prudential regulator. There may not be a clear delineation between each regulatory element; for example, adequate procedures for asset management might be important to maintain safety and soundness. **Appendix C** includes a discussion of the official ratings system that regulators apply to covered firms.

Safety and Soundness

Safety and soundness refers to a broad range of issues that relate to the health of a financial institution. Safety and soundness encompasses risk management, capital requirements, the diversification of a bank's portfolio, provisions for liquidity, allowances for loan and lease losses, concentrations of transactions with a single counterparty or in a single region, exposure to potentially expensive litigation, adequate training and expertise of management and staff, adequate procedures for internal controls, and many other issues. This section will not attempt to address all of the categories of safety and soundness regulation listed in **Table 2** above. Safety and soundness regulation is conducted prospectively—that is, banks can be examined prior to any indication of excess risk or any evidence of wrongdoing.

Safety and soundness regulation relates to economic policy issues because it can affect the credit cycle and conflicts of interest. The rapid decline in the price of one product (and thus a rapid rise in loan defaults by related firms, employees, etc.) is less likely to cause a wave of bank failures if banks are not permitted to concentrate their loan exposure to one industry or one line of business. Owners and counterparties of banks are more likely to effectively monitor bank managers if banks maintain clear and transparent systems of control.

Each loan has a variety of risk characteristics of concern to lenders and their regulators. Some of these risks can be estimated at the time the loan is issued. Credit risk, for example, is the risk that the borrower will fail to repay the principal of the loan as promised. Rising interest rates create another risk because the shorter-term interest rates that the lender often pays for its funds (e.g., deposit or CD rates) rise while the longer-term interest rates that the lender will receive from fixed-rate borrowers remain unchanged. Falling interest rates are not riskless either: fixed-rate borrowers may choose to repay loans early, reducing the lender's expected future cash flow. Federal financial regulators take into account expected default rates, prepayment rates, interest-rate exposure, and other risks when examining the loans issued by covered lenders.

The risk of a portfolio of bank assets is not just the sum of the risks of the individual loans and securities that make it up. Lenders can adjust the composition of their balance sheets to reduce or enhance the risks of the individual loans that make it up. A lender with many loans exposed to prepayment risk when interest rates fall, for example, could compensate by acquiring some assets that rise in value when interest rates fall. One example of a compensating asset would be an interest-rate derivative contract. Lenders are required to keep capital in reserve against the possibility of a drop in value of loan portfolios or other risky assets. Federal financial regulators take into account compensating assets, risk-based capital requirements, and other prudential standards when examining the balance sheets of covered lenders.

When regulators determine that a bank is taking excessive risks, or engaging in unsafe and unsound practices, they have a number of tools at their disposal to reduce risk to the institution (and ultimately to the federal deposit insurance fund). They can require banks to reduce specified lending or financing practices, dispose of certain assets, and order banks to take steps to restore sound balance sheets. In enforcement, regulators have "life-or-death" options, such as withdrawing deposit insurance, revoking the charter, or taking over a failing bank. In practice, bank regulators rarely use draconian tactics, and banks are given an opportunity to address concerns raised during an examination if the failure of the bank is not imminent.

Capital Requirements

As a general accounting concept, capital refers to the equity of a business—the amount by which its assets exceed its liabilities.[12] The more capital a firm has, the greater its capacity to absorb losses and remain solvent. Capital is related to leverage (various measures of the firm's reliance on debt and derivatives to fund its activities); firms that fund themselves with more equity capital (instead of debt) tend to have lower leverage ratios.

Capital regulation relates to economic policy problems because it can affect the credit cycle. One way higher bank capital affects the credit cycle is its potential to make the banking system more resilient during downturns. Unexpected loan losses are less likely to cause a bank to fail if it holds more capital. In the aggregate, higher capital requirements will tend to make the banking system

---

[12] Regulatory uses of "capital" include more specific definitions and classifications.

more resilient because distressed banks may drain other banks of their liquid reserves while general liquidity is declining. On the other hand, banks are part of a broader financial system, therefore it may be possible that higher capital requirements for banks might not make the system as a whole safer if the cost of capital causes more financial activity to migrate to securities markets or shadow banking.

Capital regulation can also affect the credit cycle by affecting the amount of bank credit made available. Higher bank capital requirements tend to lower the leverage that banks can achieve, which reduces the potential lending that the banking system can offer to the broader economy. Whether higher capital requirements for banks lower total lending in the economy is more difficult to determine because it depends in part on how securities markets and shadow banking react.

Financial regulators require the institutions they supervise to maintain specified minimum levels of capital—defined in various ways—to increase the resilience of firms to shocks and to minimize losses to investors, customers, and taxpayers when failures occur. The riskiness of a bank's business model affects its capital requirements; for example, a bank that specializes in relatively risky credit card lending may have higher effective capital requirements than a bank that has a relatively safer and more diversified portfolio of commercial lending. Capital requirements, if they are set above what a firm would choose on its own, represent a cost to businesses because they reduce the amount of funds that may be loaned or invested in the market. Thus, there is a perpetual tension: individual banks adjust their own capital ratio to maximize profits, whereas regulators continually modify capital standards to either prevent excessive risk-taking or to promote the availability of credit to the wider economy.

The actual capital held by banks should not be confused with statutory minimums. Banks may choose to hold excess capital if bank management believes that economic conditions may deteriorate. For example, in 2007 and 2008, JPMorgan executives referred to their portfolio as a "fortress balance sheet" in part because it was believed to be prepared for a worsening economic environment. Bank regulators may encourage regulated banks to hold additional capital to make the banking system more resilient. Following the financial turmoil of September 2008, banking regulators oversaw an increase in bank capital without the need for new legislation, new notice and comment rulemaking, or new international negotiations because bank regulators can require changes by insured depositories under existing authority (whether due to encouragement of regulators or changed preferences for prudence by bank managers).

U.S. banking regulators cooperate with banking regulators in other countries. The general approach to capital standards are based on the Basel Accords, an international framework developed under the auspices of the Bank for International Settlements.[13] Although the Basel Accords use the term *requirement*, Basel capital standards are not enforceable if a member country does not implement them (unlike the WTO dispute resolution process, for example). In other words, each participating country sets its own capital standards, but member countries use the Basel framework to establish best practices and harmonize banking regulation. The Basel committee describes its function thusly:

---

[13] See CRS Report R42744, *U.S. Implementation of the Basel Capital Regulatory Framework*, by Darryl E. Getter.

> The Basel Committee on Banking Supervision provides a forum for regular cooperation on banking supervisory matters. Its objective is to enhance understanding of key supervisory issues and improve the quality of banking supervision worldwide. It seeks to do so by exchanging information on national supervisory issues, approaches and techniques, with a view to promoting common understanding. At times, the Committee uses this common understanding to develop guidelines and supervisory standards in areas where they are considered desirable. In this regard, the Committee is best known for its international standards on capital adequacy; the Core Principles for Effective Banking Supervision; and the Concordat on cross-border banking supervision.[14]

A guiding principle of the Basel standards is that capital requirements should be risk-based. The riskier an asset, the more capital a bank should hold against possible losses. Risk-based regulations can be more prudent than simple leverage ratios because two firms with identical amounts of debt may have very different probabilities of failure if their assets are different. For example, one might lend primarily to households (credit cards, mortgages, student loans, and auto loans), whereas the other lends primarily to manufacturing businesses or agricultural service providers.

One possible drawback of a risk-based capital adequacy approach is that the regulation may become procyclical. That is, the capital standards themselves may reinforce the tendency for the banking system to expand credit during economic booms and contract credit during economic busts as views of risk evolve. If so, then risk-based capital requirements will make it more difficult for macro-prudential regulators to mitigate asset bubbles when they form, and will make it more difficult to promote additional credit expansion during economic downturns.

Procyclicality could occur if economic forecasters and financial analysts are overconfident that stable economic environments will continue or are over-pessimistic during unstable economic environments. To the extent that evaluating the risk of a long-term asset involves evaluating the probability of future economic instability, over-confidence will lead to lower than optimal capital requirements and over-pessimism will lead to higher than optimal capital requirements. If regulators and market participants are using the same financial models with similar historical data, it is unlikely that the regulators would provide much of a check on some sources of pro-cyclicality in a risk-based system because the regulators and the banks could have similar measures of risk. On the other hand, regulators could require additional stress tests for the system as a whole, which an individual firm would not have the incentive or ability to conduct.

Asset Management

Asset management refers to providing financial products or services to a third party for a fee or commission. Examples of asset management include personal fiduciary services, such as wealth management for private clients. Other examples include acting as a custodian, providing security holder services, and offering investment advice.

Regulation of asset management activities relates to economic policy issues because the asset management services of banks can have broader effects. An example of the relation of asset management to the policy issues is the custodian role of banks for some complex financial

---

[14] Bank for International Settlements, "About the Basel Committee," January 23, 2013, available at http://www.bis.org/bcbs/about.htm.

transactions. For example, some forms of interbank lending include collateral, but who will hold the collateral for the duration of the contract? If custodian banks mismanage the assets, then disruptions in interbank lending markets can be magnified during periods of financial turmoil. During financial instability, banks may be turning to collateralized lending precisely because they have greater desire for safety, certainty, and speed. Disruptions to asset management services, through either the failure of central custodian banks or slow processing of existing custodian banks, may reinforce other banks' fears of uncertainty and slow processing.

Banks are not the only firms that offer asset management services. Thus, as discussed above, bank regulators do not make rules for the entire asset management industry; rather, they issue guidance to the firms with particular charters, and they provide examinations to insure that chartered banks have procedures in place that are consistent with sound asset management principles.

Consumer Protection Compliance

Lenders must comply with a variety of statutes and regulations when offering financial products to consumers. Prior to the financial crisis, authority to oversee consumer financial protection had been spread among a number of banking regulators, HUD, and the FTC. The Dodd-Frank Act gathered much of this authority and personnel into a new Consumer Financial Protection Bureau (CFPB), but bank regulators still supervise many consumer activities of their chartered firms. One reason is that poor customer relations can be a threat to the safety and soundness of the institution, in part because it is usually bad for business. The banking agencies examine banks for compliance with consumer laws and assist in resolving consumer complaints.

Bank regulators can facilitate consumer compliance by offering an ombudsman to assist in resolving complaints. Ombudsman offices are usually separate from those of the safety and soundness examiners. Such offices may help insure that consumers receive a fair and expeditious resolution of their concerns with a firm that is regulated by that agency. This may help reduce the time and expense of more formal complaint resolution options where consumers might otherwise seek redress (such as courts).

Some rulemaking activity for consumer compliance is shared between the CFPB and the bank regulators. For example, the CFPB has issued rules for appraisals of residential properties and mortgages. However, banks also rely on appraisals to establish collateral for their mortgage loans; thus, both the CFPB and bank regulators are involved in rulemaking for residential real estate appraisals.

Regulators of Firms with Bank Charters

In many cases, depository banks are owned within a larger holding company structure, and the primary prudential regulator of the holding company may not be the same as the primary prudential regulator of the bank subsidiary. There is a dual banking system, in which each depository institution is subject to regulation by its chartering authority: state or federal. In addition, because virtually all depository institutions are covered by federal deposit insurance, they are subject to at least one federal primary regulator (i.e., the federal authority responsible for examining the institution for safety and soundness and ensuring its compliance with federal banking laws).

The federal banking agencies are briefly discussed below, along with certain powers that these agencies have that are not limited to the firms of which each is the primary prudential regulator.

Office of the Comptroller of the Currency

The Office of the Comptroller (OCC) was created in 1863 as part of the Department of the Treasury to supervise federally chartered banks (i.e., "national" banks) and to replace the circulation of state-bank notes with a single national currency (Chapter 106, 13 Stat. 99). The OCC is the primary prudential regulator for federally chartered banks and thrifts. The head of the OCC, the Comptroller of the Currency, is also a member of the board of the FDIC and a voting member of FSOC. Like the other prudential regulators described below, the OCC has examination powers to enforce its responsibilities for the safety and soundness of nationally chartered banks, and strong enforcement powers, including the ability to issue cease and desist orders and revoke the charter of covered firms.

In addition to institution-level examinations, the OCC oversees systemic risk among nationally chartered banks and thrifts. One example of OCC systemic surveillance is the regular survey of credit underwriting practices. This survey compares underwriting standards over time and assesses whether OCC examiners believe the credit risk of nationally chartered bank portfolios is rising or falling. In addition, the OCC publishes regular reports on the derivatives activities of U.S. commercial banks.

Federal Deposit Insurance Corporation

The FDIC was created in 1933 to provide assurance to small depositors that they would not lose their savings if their bank failed (P.L. 74-305, 49 Stat. 684). The FDIC is the primary federal prudential regulator of state-chartered banks that are not members of the Federal Reserve System. It has, to some extent, similar examination and enforcement powers for the firms it regulates, as the OCC has for federally chartered banks. In addition to its role as a prudential bank regulator, the FDIC administers a deposit insurance fund and resolves failing depositories and certain systemic non-banks.

Deposit insurance relates to economic policy issues because it may help to stabilize an important source of bank funding during times of financial turmoil. Prior to the 1930s, American financial crises were often accompanied by rapid withdrawal of deposits from banks rumored to be in trouble (or actually in trouble). Even prudent, well-managed banks could have difficulty surviving these runs by depositors. Federal deposit insurance assures depositors that the full-faith and credit of the federal government guarantees their deposits up to a preset level. Despite occasional periods of bank failures, banks with insured deposits have suffered almost no depositor runs since the establishment of deposit insurance. Banks are assessed premiums by the FDIC for the deposit coverage.

The agency provides deposit insurance to all federally insured banks and thrifts (but not credit unions). In 2008, as the financial crisis worsened, Congress passed a temporary increase in the deposit insurance ceiling from $100,000 to $250,000 for most accounts.[15] The increase was made permanent by the Dodd-Frank Act.

---

[15] Section 135 of the Emergency Economic Stabilization Act of 2008 (EESA; P.L. 110-343).

The deposit insurance system has been revised a number of times. For example, legislative reform (P.L. 109-173, 119 Stat. 3601) in the mid-2000s raised the coverage limit for retirement accounts to $250,000 and indexed both its limit and the general deposit insurance coverage ceiling to inflation. The reform act made changes to the risk-based assessment system to determine the payments of individual institutions. Within a range set by the reform act, the FDIC uses notice and comment rulemaking to set the designated reserve ratio (DRR) that supports the Deposit Insurance Fund (DIF). The FDIC uses its power to examine individual institutions and issue regulations for all insured-depository institutions to monitor and enforce safety and soundness.[16]

Using emergency authority it received under the Federal Deposit Insurance Corporation Improvement Act of 1991 (FDICIA; P.L. 102-242),[17] the FDIC made a determination of systemic risk in October 2008 and announced that it would temporarily guarantee (1) newly issued senior unsecured debt of banks, thrifts, and certain holding companies and (2) non-interest bearing deposit transaction accounts (e.g., business checking accounts), regardless of dollar amount.[18] Under Dodd-Frank, the FDIC's authority to guarantee bank debt is made explicit. Although the 2008 emergency measures have expired, the FDIC has the authority to create some programs during a possible future crisis.

The financial crisis of 2008 revealed a number of lessons related to bank runs and deposit insurance. Several non-banks suffered the equivalent of depositor runs, including money market mutual funds and the interbank repo market. Because the equivalent of depositor runs can occur in other financial activities, Dodd-Frank expanded the assessment base for FDIC premiums to include a bank's entire balance sheet, not just its insured deposits. Furthermore, creditors of failing financial institutions may, under extreme circumstances, be provided with additional guarantees if the failure is determined to be a threat to the financial stability of the United States.

When banks fail, the FDIC disposes the assets and liabilities. The FDIC manages the DIF, which is derived from risk-based assessments levied on depository institutions. The fund is used for various purposes, primarily for resolving failed or failing institutions. The FDIC has broad jurisdiction because nearly all banks and thrifts, whether federally or state-chartered, carry FDIC insurance.

The Dodd-Frank Act also expanded the FDIC's role in liquidating troubled financial institutions. Under the act, the Financial Stability Oversight Council (FSOC) will designate certain financial institutions—banks and nonbanks—as systemically important. In addition to more stringent capital regulation, those firms are required to draw up "living wills," or plans for orderly liquidation. The Federal Reserve, with the concurrence of two-thirds of the FSOC, may determine that a firm represents a "severe threat" to financial stability and may order it closed. The FDIC will administer the resolution process for nonbanks as well as banks.[19]

---

[16] CRS Report R41718, *Federal Deposit Insurance for Banks and Credit Unions*, by Darryl E. Getter.

[17] FDICIA created a new Section 13(c)(4) of the Federal Deposit Insurance Act, 12 USC §1823(c)(4)(G).

[18] FDIC, "FDIC Announces Plan to Free Up Bank Liquidity," press release, October 14, 2008, http://www.fdic.gov/news/news/press/2008/pr08100.html.

[19] For more detail, see CRS Report R41384, *The Dodd-Frank Wall Street Reform and Consumer Protection Act: Systemic Risk and the Federal Reserve*, by Marc Labonte.

The Federal Reserve

The Federal Reserve System was established in 1913 to provide stability to banks and trusts through the regulation of reserves (P.L. 63-43, 38 STAT. 251). The Federal Reserve System has three components: the Federal Reserve Board (FRB), the regional Federal Reserve Banks (FRBNY, FRBSF, etc.), and the Open Market Committee. The Fed is the primary prudential regulator for a variety of lending institutions, including bank holding companies, certain U.S. branches of foreign banks, and state-chartered banks that are members of the Federal Reserve System. Under the Gramm-Leach-Bliley Act (GLBA; P.L. 106-102), the Fed serves as the umbrella regulator for financial holding companies, which are defined as conglomerates that are permitted to engage in a broad array of financially related activities. As a primary prudential regulator, the Federal Reserve has similar authority as the OCC.

In addition to the charter class that the Federal Reserve regulates, the Dodd-Frank Act made the Fed the primary regulator of all financial firms (bank or nonbank) that are designated as systemically significant by the FSOC (of which the Fed is a member). Capital requirements for such firms may be stricter than for other firms. In addition, Dodd-Frank made the Fed the principal regulator for systemically important financial-market utilities. The Fed also regulates savings and loan holding companies and securities holding companies, formerly defined in securities law as an investment bank holding company.

In addition to its powers as a primary prudential regulator, the Federal Reserve conducts monetary policy, monitors the financial system, acts as the fiscal agent of the United States, and regulates the payment system and a number of financial activities. Examples of additional activities regulated by the Fed (sometimes only as a monitor and sometimes jointly with other agencies) include equal credit opportunity (Reg-B), Community Reinvestment Act (CRA) related agreements (Reg-G), and extensions of credit by brokers and dealers (Reg-T). The list of regulatory topics now extends from Reg-A to Reg-YY.

National Credit Union Administration

The National Credit Union Administration (NCUA), originally part of the Farm Credit Administration, became an independent agency in 1970 (P.L. 91-206, 84 STAT. 49). The NCUA regulates all federal credit unions and those state credit unions that elect to be federally insured. It administers a Central Liquidity Facility, which is the credit union lender of last resort, and the National Credit Union Share Insurance Fund, which insures credit union deposits. Credit unions are member-owned financial cooperatives and must be not-for-profit institutions. As cooperatives, they are exempt from corporate income tax. Many credit unions offer similar services as community banks, and this differential tax treatment is often the subject of legislative proposals in each congressional session.

Regulating Securities, Derivatives, and Other Contract Markets

Regulators of financial trading attempt to address many economic policy problems. As discussed in the introductory sections, financial markets may not be level playing fields—some people with access to confidential information may have a trading advantage. Furthermore, the people who issue and market new securities (or derivatives) may have the incentive to withhold or mischaracterize some of the information they have about the securities or derivatives being offered. Even if these market facilitators provide full information, the outcome might still be less than optimal if other market participants simply believe that material information is not being disclosed or that insiders are behaving strategically. As a result, much of the regulation of securities and derivatives markets has focused on resolving conflicts of interest and requiring full disclosure of material information, unlike bank regulation that tends to focus on prudence. In addition, much securities market regulation has been applied through enforcement against after-the-fact violations, rather than as prospective examinations of covered firms.

Non-Bank Financial Regulators

Securities and Exchange Commission

The SEC was created as an independent agency in 1934 to enforce newly written federal securities laws (P.L. 73-291, 48 Stat. 881). Although the SEC is concerned with ensuring the safety and soundness of the firms it regulates, its primary concern is maintaining fair and orderly markets and protecting investors from fraud. The SEC generally[20] does not have the authority to limit risks taken by non-bank financial institutions or the ability to prop up a failing firm, with some exceptions. Two types of firms come under the SEC's jurisdiction: (1) all corporations that sell securities to the public and (2) securities broker/dealers and other securities markets intermediaries.

Firms that sell securities—stocks and bonds—to the public are required to register with the SEC. Registration entails the publication of detailed information about the firm, its management, the intended uses for the funds raised through the sale of securities, and the risks to investors. The initial registration disclosures must be kept current through the filing of periodic financial statements: annual and quarterly reports (as well as special reports when there is a material change in the firm's financial condition or prospects).

Beyond these disclosure requirements, and certain other rules that apply to corporate governance, the SEC does not have any direct regulatory control over publicly traded firms. Bank regulators are expected to identify unsafe and unsound banking practices in the institutions they supervise and have the power to intervene and prevent banks from taking excessive risks. The SEC has no comparable authority; the securities laws simply require that risks be disclosed to investors. Registration with the SEC, in other words, is in no sense a government endorsement that a security is a good or safe investment.

To enable investors to make informed investment choices, the SEC has statutory authority over financial accounting standards. All publicly traded firms are required to use generally accepted accounting principles (GAAP), which are formulated by the Financial Accounting Standards Board (FASB), the American Institute of Certified Public Accountants (AICPA), and the SEC itself.

Besides publicly traded corporations, a number of securities market participants are also required to register with the SEC (or with one of the industry self-regulatory organizations that the SEC oversees). These include stock exchanges, securities brokerages (and numerous classes of their

---

[20] A counter example would be SEC's net capital rule as discussed below in "The SEC's Net Capital Rule."

personnel), mutual funds, auditors, investment advisers, and others. To maintain their registered status, all these entities must comply with rules meant to protect investors' interests, prevent fraud, and promote fair and orderly markets. The area of SEC supervision most analogous to banking regulation is broker/dealer regulation. Several provisions of law and regulation protect brokerage customers from losses arising from brokerage firm failure. The Securities Investor Protection Corporation (SIPC), created by Congress in 1970, operates an insurance scheme funded by assessments on broker/dealers (and with a backup line of credit with the U.S. Treasury). SIPC guarantees customer accounts up to $500,000 for losses arising from brokerage failure or fraud (but not market losses). Unlike the FDIC, however, SIPC does not examine broker/dealers and has no regulatory powers.

Since 1975, the SEC has enforced a net capital rule applicable to all registered broker/dealers. The rule requires broker/dealers to maintain an excess of capital above mere solvency, to ensure that a failing firm stops trading while it still has assets to meet customer claims. Net capital levels are calculated in a manner similar to the risk-based capital requirements under the Basel Accords, but the SEC has its own set of risk weightings, which it calls "haircuts." The riskier the asset, the greater the haircut.

Although the net capital rule appears to be similar in its effects to the banking agencies' risk-based capital requirements, there are significant differences. The SEC has no authority to intervene in a broker/dealer's business if it takes excessive risks that might cause net capital to drop below the required level. Rather, the net capital rule is often described as a liquidation rule—not meant to prevent failures but to minimize the impact on customers. Moreover, the SEC has no authority comparable to the banking regulators' prompt corrective action powers: it cannot preemptively seize a troubled broker/dealer or compel it to merge with a sound firm.

The differences between bank and securities regulation with respect to safety and soundness came into sharp focus with the collapse of Bear Stearns, one of the five largest investment banks, in March 2008.[21] The SEC monitored Bear Stearns' financial condition until shortly before the collapse (which was precipitated by the refusal of other market participants to extend short-term credit to Bear Stearns), and it believed that the firm had sufficient levels of capital and liquidity. When bankruptcy suddenly loomed, it was the Federal Reserve that stepped in to broker the sale of Bear Stearns to JP Morgan Chase by agreeing to purchase $30 billion of "toxic" Bear Stearns assets.

The Bear Stearns situation highlighted several apparent anomalies in the U.S. regulatory structure. The SEC lacked safety and soundness powers over the institutions it supervised, and the Fed was forced to commit funds to an investment bank over which it had no regulatory jurisdiction. The anomaly became even more pronounced when the Fed subsequently established a lending facility to provide short-term credit to other investment banks.[22]

The Bear Stearns collapse showed the inability of the SEC to respond to a brokerage failure with systemic risk implications. There is more to the story, however, than the differences between bank regulation and the SEC's net capital rule. In 2004, the SEC devised a voluntary supervisory scheme for the largest investment banks, called the Consolidated Supervised Entities (CSE)

---

[21] See CRS Report RL34420, *Bear Stearns: Crisis and "Rescue" for a Major Provider of Mortgage-Related Products*, by Gary Shorter.

[22] See CRS Report RL34427, *Financial Turmoil: Federal Reserve Policy Responses*, by Marc Labonte.

program.[23] The CSE firms were all registered broker/dealers, but were also large holding companies with extensive operations carried on outside the broker/dealer unit. Thus, the SEC had no capital requirement that applied to the entire investment bank. Under CSE, this was to change: as a substitute for the net capital rule, the firms agreed to abide by the Basel risk-based standard and maintain that level of capital *at the holding company level*. On a voluntary basis, the firms agreed to grant the SEC the authority to examine and monitor their compliance, above and beyond the SEC's explicit statutory authority.[24]

Whatever the intent of the CSE program, it did not succeed in preventing excessive risk-taking by the participants.[25] By the end of September 2008, all five CSE investment banks had either failed (Lehman Brothers), merged to prevent failure (Merrill Lynch and Bear Stearns), or applied for bank holding company status (Morgan Stanley and Goldman Sachs).[26] On September 26, 2008, SEC Chairman Cox announced the end of the CSE program, declaring that "[t]he last six months have made it abundantly clear that voluntary regulation does not work. When Congress passed the Gramm-Leach-Bliley Act, it created a significant regulatory gap by failing to give to the SEC or any agency the authority to regulate large investment bank holding companies."[27]

With the Dodd-Frank Act, Congress eliminated the investment bank holding company framework in Section 17 of the Securities Exchange Act of 1934. Section 618 of Dodd-Frank permits a securities holding company to be subject to consolidated supervision and submit to Federal Reserve regulation. Under Title I of Dodd-Frank, any securities firm that is deemed by the FSOC to be systemically significant will automatically come under the consolidated supervision of the Federal Reserve.

Other provisions of Dodd-Frank, however, gave the SEC new responsibilities that have aspects of safety and soundness regulation. Under Section 731, the SEC sets capital requirements for major security-based swap participants and security-based swap dealers. Section 956 gives the SEC new authority to prohibit compensation structures in broker/dealers and investment advisory firms that create inappropriate risks.

Commodity Futures Trading Commission

The CFTC was created in 1974 to regulate commodities futures and options markets, which at the time were poised to expand beyond their traditional base in agricultural commodities to encompass contracts based on financial variables, such as interest rates and stock indexes. The

---

[23] SEC, "Holding Company Supervision Program Description: Consolidated Supervised Entities ("CSEs")," http://www.sec.gov/divisions/marketreg/hcsupervision.htm.

[24] The Market Reform Act of 1990 permits the SEC to collect certain financial information from unregulated affiliates of broker/dealers, under the Broker-Dealer Risk Assessment Program. The impetus for the CSE program was a European Union requirement that investment banks operating in Europe be subject to consolidated financial supervision.

[25] Some argue that CSE allowed the investment banks to hold less capital and increase their leverage. For two views on this issue, see Stephen Labaton, "Agency's '04 Rule Let Banks Pile Up New Debt, and Risk," *New York Times*, October 3, 2008, p. A1, and Testimony of SEC Chairman Christopher Cox, House Oversight and Government Reform Committee, October 23, 2008. (Response to question from Rep. Christopher Shays.)

[26] By becoming bank holding companies, Morgan Stanley and Goldman Sachs placed themselves under Federal Reserve regulation, presumably to signal to the markets that their financial condition was being monitored and to gain access to the Fed's lending facilities.

[27] SEC, "Chairman Cox Announces End of Consolidated Supervised Entities Program," press release 2008-230.

CFTC's mission is to prevent excessive speculation, manipulation of commodity prices, and fraud. Like the SEC, the CFTC oversees industry self-regulatory organizations (SROs)—the futures exchanges and the National Futures Association—and requires the registration of a range of industry firms and personnel, including futures commission merchants (brokers), floor traders, commodity pool operators, and commodity trading advisers.

The Dodd-Frank Act greatly expanded the CFTC's jurisdiction by eliminating exemptions for certain over-the-counter derivatives. As a result, swap dealers, major swap participants, swap clearing organizations, swap execution facilities, and swap data repositories are required to register with the CFTC. These entities are subject to business conduct standards contained in statute or promulgated as CFTC rules.

Like the SEC, the CFTC does not directly regulate the safety and soundness of individual firms, with the exception of newly regulated swap dealers and major swap participants, for whom it sets capital standards pursuant to Dodd-Frank.

Federal Housing Finance Agency

The FHFA was created in 2008 by the Housing and Economic Recovery Act of 2008 (P.L. 110-289) to consolidate and strengthen regulation of a group of housing finance-related government-sponsored enterprises (GSEs): Fannie Mae, Freddie Mac, and the Federal Home Loan Banks.[28] The FHFA succeeded the Office of Federal Housing Enterprise Oversight (OFHEO) and the Federal Housing Finance Board (FHFB). FHFA authority includes both the safety and soundness authority of the former OFHEO and the housing mission goals for the GSEs that had been administered by HUD.

The impetus to create the FHFA came from concerns about risk—including systemic risk—arising from the rapid growth of the GSEs, particularly Fannie and Freddie. These two GSEs were profit-seeking, shareholder-owned corporations that took advantage of their government-sponsored status to accumulate undiversified investment portfolios of more than $1.5 trillion, consisting almost exclusively of home mortgages (and securities and derivatives based on those mortgages).

The FHFA was given enhanced safety and soundness powers resembling those of the federal bank regulators. These powers included the ability to set capital standards, order the enterprises to cease any activity or divest any asset that posed a threat to financial soundness, and replace management and assume control of the firms that became seriously undercapitalized.

One of the FHFA's first actions was to place both Fannie and Freddie in "voluntary" conservatorship.[29] Fannie and Freddie continue to operate, under an agreement with the U.S. Treasury. The Treasury provided capital to the two firms, by means of preferred stock purchases, to ensure that each remains solvent. In return, the government received warrants equivalent to a 79.9% equity ownership position in the firms.

---

[28] For more on GSEs and their regulation, see CRS Reports CRS Report R40800, *GSEs and the Government's Role in Housing Finance: Issues for the 113th Congress*, by N. Eric Weiss.

[29] See CRS Report R42760, *Fannie Mae's and Freddie Mac's Financial Status: Frequently Asked Questions*, by N. Eric Weiss.

Consumer Financial Protection Bureau

Title X of Dodd-Frank created the Consumer Financial Protection Bureau (CFPB) to bring the consumer protection regulation of depository and non-depository financial institutions into closer alignment.[30] The bureau is an independent entity within the Federal Reserve with authority over an array of consumer financial products and services (including deposit taking, mortgages, credit cards and other extensions of credit, loan servicing, check guaranteeing, collection of consumer report data, debt collection, real estate settlement, money transmitting, and financial data processing). CFPB serves as the primary federal consumer financial protection supervisor and enforcer of federal consumer protection laws over many of the institutions that offer these products and services.

However, the bureau's regulatory authority varies based on institution size and type. Regulatory authority differs for (1) depository institutions with more than $10 billion in assets, (2) depository institutions with $10 billion or less in assets, and (3) non-depositories. The Dodd-Frank Act also explicitly exempts a number of different entities and consumer financial activities from the bureau's supervisory and enforcement authority. Among the exempt entities are

- merchants, retailers, or sellers of nonfinancial goods or services, to the extent that they extend credit directly to consumers exclusively for the purpose of enabling consumers to purchase such nonfinancial goods or services;
- automobile dealers;
- real estate brokers and agents;
- financial intermediaries registered with the SEC or CFTC;
- insurance companies; and
- depository institutions with $10 billion or less in assets.

Regulatory Umbrella Groups

The need for coordination and data sharing among regulators has led to the formation of innumerable interagency task forces to study particular market episodes and make recommendations to Congress. Three interagency organizations have permanent status.

Financial Stability Oversight Council

Title I of the Dodd-Frank Act created the FSOC on the date of enactment.[31] The council is chaired by the Secretary of the Treasury, and the other voting members consist of the heads of the Federal Reserve, FDIC, OCC, NCUA, SEC, CFTC, FHFA, CFPB, and a member with insurance expertise appointed by the President. Nonvoting members, serving in an advisory capacity, include the director of the Office of Financial Research (created by Title I to support the FSOC),

---

[30] See CRS Report R41338, *The Dodd-Frank Wall Street Reform and Consumer Protection Act: Title X, The Consumer Financial Protection Bureau*, by David H. Carpenter. CRS Report R42615, *A Brief Overview of Actions Taken by the Consumer Financial Protection Bureau (CFPB) in Its First Year*, by Sean M. Hoskins.

[31] See CRS Report R41384, *The Dodd-Frank Wall Street Reform and Consumer Protection Act: Systemic Risk and the Federal Reserve*, by Marc Labonte.

the head of the Federal Insurance Office (created by Title V of Dodd-Frank), a state banking supervisor, a state insurance commissioner, and a state securities commissioner.

The FSOC is tasked with identifying risks to financial stability and responding to emerging systemic risks, while minimizing moral hazard arising from expectations that firms or their counterparties will be rescued from failure. The FSOC's duties include

- collecting information on financial firms from regulators and through the Office of Financial Research;
- monitoring the financial system to identify potential systemic risks;
- proposing regulatory changes to Congress to promote stability, competitiveness, and efficiency;
- facilitating information sharing and coordination among financial regulators;
- making regulatory recommendations to financial regulators, including "new or heightened standards and safeguards";
- identifying gaps in regulation that could pose systemic risk;
- reviewing and commenting on new or existing accounting standards issued by any standard-setting body; and
- providing a forum for the resolution of jurisdictional disputes among council members. The FSOC may not impose any resolution on disagreeing members, however.

The council is required to provide an annual report and testimony to Congress.

In contrast to some proposals to create a systemic risk regulator, the Dodd-Frank Act does not give the council authority (beyond the existing authority of its individual members) to eliminate emerging threats or close regulatory gaps it identifies. In most cases, the council can only make regulatory recommendations—it cannot impose change.

Although the FSOC does not have direct supervisory authority over any financial institution, it plays an important role in regulation, because firms that it designates as systemically important come under a consolidated supervisory regime that may be considerably more stringent than the standards that apply to non-systemic firms. The FSOC is also required to approve (by a two-thirds vote) decisions by the Federal Reserve to shut down systemically significant financial firms that pose a severe threat to financial stability.

Federal Financial Institution Examinations Council

The Federal Financial Institutions Examination Council (FFIEC) was created by legislation[32] in 1979 as a formal interagency body to coordinate federal regulation of lending institutions. Through the FFIEC, the federal banking regulators issue a single set of reporting forms for covered institutions. The FFIEC also attempts to harmonize auditing principles and supervisory decisions. The FFIEC is made up of the Federal Reserve, OCC, FDIC, NCUA, and CFPB. Except

---

[32] P.L. 95-630, 92 STAT. 3641.

for the CFPB, the member agencies of the FFIEC are primary prudential regulators of depository institutions with specific charters as described above and employ examiners to enforce safety and soundness regulations for lending institutions. The examination powers of the CFPB for compliance with consumer protection rules varies across institutions, many of which may not have bank charters.

Federal financial institution examiners evaluate the risks of covered institutions. The specific safety and soundness concerns common to the FFIEC agencies can be found in the examiner's handbook to monitor lenders. Each subject area of the handbook can be updated separately. Examples of safety and soundness subject areas include important indicators of risk, such as capital adequacy, asset quality, liquidity, and sensitivity to market risk.

President's Working Group on Financial Markets

The President's Working Group on Financial Markets (PWG) was created by President Reagan through executive order in 1988.[33] The PWG includes the Secretary of the Treasury and the Chairmen of the Federal Reserve, the SEC, and the CFTC. It is not a formal agency subject to congressional oversight, although each member is subject to Senate confirmation at the time of appointment.

The impetus for the creation of the PWG was the stock market crash of October 1987, and specifically the role that the stock index futures markets (under CFTC jurisdiction) played in creating panic in the stock market (regulated by SEC). Studies conducted by the SEC, the CFTC, a blue-ribbon panel appointed by the President (the Presidential Task Force on Market Mechanisms, or Brady Commission), and the stock and futures exchanges reached strikingly different conclusions; the task of the PWG was to review the studies and issue a further report.

The PWG provides interagency coordination and information sharing and studies entities and products that raise intermarket regulatory issues, such as hedge funds and OTC derivatives. For example, in March 2008, the PWG issued a policy statement on the ongoing financial crisis.[34] Another example is the October 2010 PWG report called for changes to address systemic risk and reduce the susceptibility of money market mutual funds (MMFs) to runs.[35]

Non-Bank Capital Requirements

Federal Housing Finance Agency

The Federal Housing Finance Agency (FHFA) is authorized to set capital classification standards for the Federal Home Loan Banks, Fannie Mae, and Freddie Mac that reflect the differences in operations between the banks and the latter two GSEs.[36] The law defines several capital

---

[33] Executive Order 12631, March 18, 1988, 53 FR 9421.

[34] President's Working Group on Financial Markets, "Policy Statement on Financial Market Developments," March 2008, http://www.ustreas.gov/press/releases/reports/pwgpolicystatemktturmoil_03122008.pdf.

[35] Securities and Exchange Commission, "President's Working Group Report on Money Market Fund Reform," Release No. IC-29497; File No. 4-619, available at http://www.sec.gov/rules/other/2010/ic-29497.pdf.

[36] See Sections 1142 and 1143 of the Housing and Economic Recovery Act of 2008, P.L. 110-289.

classifications and prescribes regulatory actions to be taken as a GSE's condition worsens. Limitations are placed on a GSE if it does not meet certain capital standards.

No growth in total assets is permitted for an *undercapitalized* GSE, unless (1) FHFA has accepted the GSE's capital restoration plan, (2) an increase in assets is consistent with the plan, and (3) the ratios of both total capital to assets and tangible equity to assets are increasing. An undercapitalized entity is subject to heightened scrutiny and supervision.

If a regulated entity is *significantly undercapitalized*, FHFA must take one or more of the following actions: elect new directors, dismiss directors or executives, and hire qualified executive officers, or other actions. Without prior written approval, executives of a significantly undercapitalized regulated entity may not receive bonuses or pay raises. In addition, FHFA may appoint a receiver or conservator for several specified causes related to financial difficulty or violations of law or regulation.

When a GSE becomes *critically undercapitalized*, receivership or conservatorship provisions apply. For example, FHFA must appoint itself as the receiver if a regulated entity's assets are (and have been for 60 days) less than its obligations to its creditors, or if the regulated entity has (for 60 days) not been generally paying its debts as they come due. Although both GSEs were technically adequately capitalized according to the March 2008 FHFA report, both firms were experiencing losses large enough to threaten continued solvency. In July 2008, Congress empowered Treasury to provide financial assistance to the GSEs, and the FHFA appointed itself conservator for both Fannie and Freddie in September 2008, before either GSE had failed to make timely payments on debt obligations.

FHFA may downgrade the capital classification of a regulated entity (1) whose conduct could rapidly deplete core or total capital, or (in the case of Fannie or Freddie) whose mortgage assets have declined significantly in value, (2) that is determined (after notice and opportunity for a hearing) to be in an unsafe or unsound condition, or (3) that is engaging in an unsafe or unsound practice.

The SEC's Net Capital Rule

The SEC's net capital rule, set out in 17 CFR 240.15c3-1, imposes an "Aggregate Indebtedness Standard." No broker/dealer shall permit its aggregate indebtedness to all other persons to exceed 1500% of its net capital (or 800% of its net capital for 12 months after commencing business as a broker or dealer).[37] The 1500% (or 15-to-1) ratio of debt to liquid capital, is arithmetically equivalent to a 6⅔% capital requirement.

To calculate liquid capital, SEC rules require that securities and other assets be given a "haircut" from their current market values (or face value, in the case of bonds), to cover the risk that the asset's value might decline before it could be sold. The haircut concept—the riskier the asset, the greater the haircut—is essentially the same as the standardized risk weights in the Basel Accords. For example, U.S. Treasury securities might have a lower haircut than municipal securities, which might have a lower haircut than corporate bonds, which in turn might have a lower haircut than common stock. Certain assets, such as unsecured receivables or securities for which no ready

---

[37] This is an example of the SEC regulation for the risk that a firm takes, as alluded to in the description of the SEC.

market exists, receive a haircut of 100%. The Dodd-Frank Act requires the SEC to set capital standards for major security-based swap dealers and major security-based swap participants.

CFTC Capital Requirements

Futures commission merchants (or FCMs, the futures equivalent of a securities broker/dealer) are subject to adjusted net capital requirements. Authority to enforce the capital rules is delegated by the CFTC to the National Futures Association (NFA), a self-regulatory organization created by Congress.

Each NFA member that is required to be registered with the CFTC as a futures commission merchant (member FCM) must maintain "Adjusted Net Capital" (as defined in CFTC Regulation 1.17) equal to or in excess of the greatest of

> (i) $500,000;

> (ii) For Member FCMs with less than $2,000,000 in Adjusted Net Capital, $6,000 for each remote location operated;

> (iii) For Member FCMs with less than $2,000,000 in Adjusted Net Capital, $3,000 for each associated person;

> (iv) For securities brokers and dealers, the amount of net capital specified by SEC regulations;

> (v) 8% of domestic and foreign domiciled customer and 4% of non-customer (excluding proprietary) risk maintenance margin/performance bond requirements for all domestic and foreign futures and options on futures contracts excluding the risk margin associated with naked long option positions;

> (vi) For Member FCMs with an affiliate that engages in foreign exchange (FX) transactions and that is authorized to engage in those transactions solely by virtue of its affiliation with a registered FCM, $7,500,000; or

> (vii) For Member FCMs that are counterparties to FX options, $5,000,000, except that FX Dealer Members must meet the higher requirement in Financial Requirements Section 11.[38]

The Dodd-Frank Act defines several categories of major derivatives participants and requires the CFTC to set capital standards for major security-based swap dealers and major security-based swap participants.

Foreign Exchange Markets

Buying and selling currencies is essential to foreign trade, and the exchange rate has major implications for a country's macroeconomic policy. Although the United States allows its currency to float, the foreign exchange market is not completely free because of the actions of central banks. For example, the central banks of other countries may seek to peg their currency to

---

[38] National Futures Association, *NFA Manual/Rules*, Section 7001, http://www.nfa.futures.org/nfaManual/manualFinancial.asp#fins1.

the dollar. The market is one of the largest in the world, with average daily foreign exchange turnover in excess of $4 trillion.[39] Federal Reserve monetary policies affect the value of the dollar (even if the Fed does not intentionally target the value of the dollar), but no agency is granted sole authority to regulate the mechanics of foreign exchange trading, except to the extent foreign exchange futures are offered on regulated exchanges.

Trading in currencies takes place between large global banks, central banks, hedge funds and other currency speculators, commercial firms involved in imports and exports, fund managers, and retail brokers. Currency trading is largely conducted in the over-the-counter market.

U.S. Treasury Securities

Like the foreign exchange market, there is no central exchange for the resale market for U.S. Treasuries, but there are a number of proprietary, computer-based transaction systems. Treasury securities were exempted from SEC regulation by the original securities laws of the 1930s and under the Volcker Rule in the Dodd-Frank Act. In 1993, following a successful corner of a Treasury bond auction by Salomon Brothers, Congress passed the Government Securities Act Amendments (P.L. 103-202), which required brokers and dealers in government securities that were not already registered with the SEC to register as government securities dealers. (Existing broker/dealer registrants were simply required to notify the SEC that they were in the government securities business.) Nevertheless, the government securities market remains much more lightly regulated than the corporate securities markets.

The primary market in Treasury securities, in which new debt instruments are sold to fund government operations, is monitored by the Federal Reserve Bank of New York (FRBNY). A principal channel for the distribution of new Treasuries is a group of firms called primary dealers, who purchase securities at auction for their own accounts and for their customers. The primary dealers are 19 commercial and investment banks, both foreign and domestic. The primary dealer list is maintained by the FRBNY, which also issues a list of practices that it expects primary dealers to comply with. FRBNY conducts auctions for the Treasury, but its relationship to the dealers is commercial, rather than providing prudential regulation.[40] The New York Fed does, however, collect certain data about primary dealers' transactions in government securities.

In March 2008, as part of its multifaceted attempt to supply liquidity to the financial system, the Federal Reserve established a Primary Dealer Credit Facility, to make short-term loans against a variety of collateral (including asset-backed and mortgage-backed securities) to the primary dealers.[41] This step attracted attention in part because the primary dealer group included investment banking firms of which the Fed had no regulatory authority.

---

[39] Bank for International Settlements, *Triennial Central Bank Survey of Foreign Exchange and Derivatives Market Activity*, September 2010, http://www.bis.org/publ/rpfxf10t.htm.

[40] See http://www.newyorkfed.org/aboutthefed/fedpoint/fed02.html.

[41] Federal Reserve Bank of New York, "Federal Reserve Announces Establishment of Primary Dealer Credit Facility," Press Release, March 16, 2008, http://www.newyorkfed.org/newsevents/news/markets/2008/rp080316.html.

Private Securities Markets

The securities laws mandate registration of, and extensive disclosures by, public securities issuers, but also provide for private sales of securities, which are not subject to disclosure requirements. Private placements of securities may only be offered to limited numbers of "accredited investors" who meet certain asset tests. (Most purchasers are life insurers and other institutional investors.) There are also restrictions on the resale of private securities.

The size of the private placement market is subject to considerable variation from year to year, but at times the value of securities sold privately exceeds what is sold into the public market. In recent decades, venture capitalists and private equity firms have come to play important roles in corporate finance. The former typically purchase interests in private firms, which may be sold later to the public, while the latter often purchase all the stock of publicly traded companies and take them private.

Appendix A. Capital Requirements: Provisions in Dodd-Frank

The Dodd-Frank Act includes numerous provisions that seek to strengthen capital requirements of banks and to extend capital regulatory approaches to certain non-bank financial firms and markets. The general thrust of these provisions is that systemically significant firms, derivatives trading platforms, and other financial market utilities should be required to hold extra capital to compensate for the risk that their failure might pose to the system at large. Title I requires banking regulators to establish minimum risk-based capital requirements and leverage requirements on a consolidated basis for depository institutions, depository holding companies, and firms designated by the Financial Stability Oversight Council (FSOC) as systemically significant. These requirements must be no lower than those that were set for depository institutions as of the date of enactment (July 2010). One example of the effect of this provision is that bank holding companies will no longer be able to include trust-preferred securities in Tier I capital. These requirements are phased in over time, and certain small firms are exempted.

Section 115(c) requires the Financial Stability Oversight Council to study the feasibility of implementing a contingent capital requirement for systemically significant firms. Contingent capital is debt that can be converted into equity by the issuing firm under certain circumstances. Following the study, if the FSOC recommends, the Fed may impose contingent capital requirements on systemically significant firms.

Section 165(j) requires the Federal Reserve to impose leverage limits on bank holding companies with assets over $50 billion and on the systemically important non-bank financial companies that it will supervise. When this section is implemented, such firms will be required to maintain a debt-to-equity ratio of no more than 15-to-1.

Title VI requires the federal banking regulators to make capital "requirements countercyclical, so that the amount of capital required to be maintained ... increases in times of economic expansion and decreases in times of economic contraction, consistent with ... safety and soundness."[42]

---

[42] Dodd-Frank Act, Section 616.

Table A-1. Capital Standards for Federally Regulated Depository Institutions

Agency	Capital Standard	Source
OCC (bank charters)	Minimum risk-based capital ratio of 8%. (The ratio measures bank capital against assets, with asset values risk-weighted, or adjusted on a scale of riskiness.) In addition, banks must maintain Tier 1 capital[a] in an amount equal to at least 3.0% of adjusted total assets. (A simple definition of Tier 1 capital is stockholders' equity, or the net worth of the institution.) The 3% total assets leverage ratio applies to the most highly rated banks, which are expected to have well-diversified risks, including no undue interest rate risk exposure, excellent control systems, good earnings, high asset quality, high liquidity, and well managed on-and off-balance sheet activities. In general, they should be considered strong banking organizations, with a rating of 1 under CAMELS[b] rating system of banks. For other banks, the minimum Tier 1 leverage ratio is 4%.	12 CFR §3.6 ("Minimum capital ratios")
FDIC	The FDIC requires institutions to maintain the same minimum leverage capital requirements (ratio of Tier 1 capital to assets) as the OCC, that is, 3% for the most highly rated institutions and 4% for others.	12 CFR §325.3 ("Minimum leverage capital requirement")
Federal Reserve	State banks that are members of the Federal Reserve System must meet an 8% risk-weighted capital standard, of which at least 4% must be Tier 1 capital (3% for strong banking institutions rated "1" under the CAMELS rating system of banks). In addition, the Fed establishes levels of reserves that depository institutions are required to maintain as part of monetary policies. Changing reserve requirements could also affect potential bank lending in a way analogous to changing capital requirements. These reserves include vault cash (currency) or deposits at the nearest regional Federal Reserve branch, held against the bank's deposit liabilities, primarily checking, saving, and time deposits (CDs). The size of these reserves places a ceiling on the amount of deposits that financial institutions can have outstanding, and ties deposit liabilities to the amount of assets (loans) these institutions can acquire.	12 CFR §208.4, Regulation H ("Membership of State Banking Institutions in the Federal Reserve System") and 12 CFR §204.9 (Reserve requirements)
OCC (thrift charters)	Risk-based capital must be at least 8% of risk-weighted assets. Federal statute requires that thrift capital regulations be no less stringent than the OCC's regulations for banks. Tangible capital must exceed 1.5% of adjusted total assets. The leverage ratio (Tier 1 capital to assets) must be 4% of adjusted total assets (3% for thrifts with a composite CAMELS rating of 1).	12 CFR §167
NCUA	Credit unions must maintain a risk-based net worth of 7%, as a minimum to be considered well capitalized.	NCUA Regulations (Section 702, Subpart A)

Source: CRS from statutes and legislation.

a. Tier 1 capital or core capital means the sum of common stockholders' equity, noncumulative perpetual preferred stock, and minority interests in consolidated subsidiaries, minus all intangible assets, minus identified losses, minus investments in certain financial subsidiaries, and minus the amount of the total adjusted carrying value of nonfinancial equity investments that is subject to a deduction from Tier 1 capital.

b. See **Appendix C** for a broader discussion of the CAMELS rating system.

Appendix B. Forms of Banking Organizations

The structure of banks can be complex. Currently, the regulator of a particular activity of a bank or its subsidiary depends in part on the activity of the subsidiary or its charter, as described previously. The following flow charts provide simplified representations of various bank structures. In some cases, the umbrella bank and its subsidiaries may have different regulators.

Figure B-1. National Bank

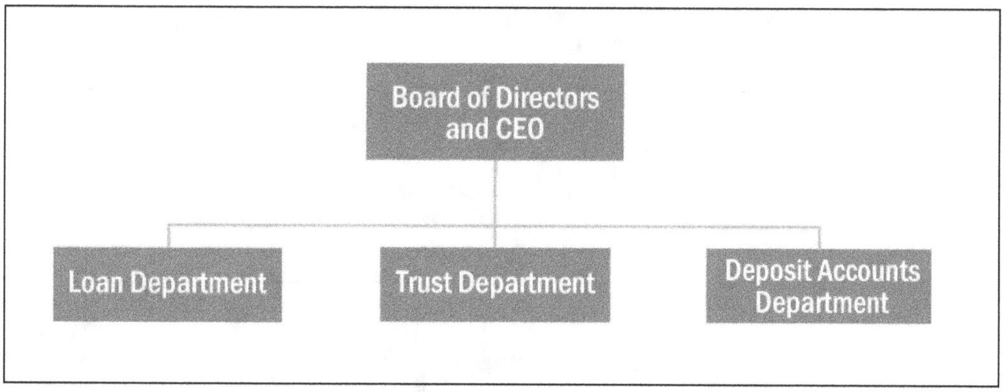

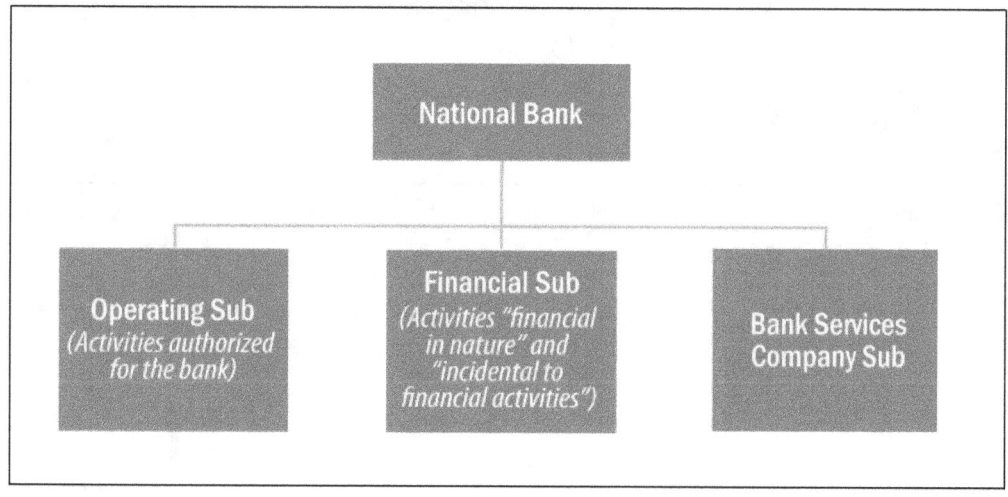

Source: The Congressional Research Service (CRS).

Figure B-2. National Bank and Subsidiaries

Source: CRS.

Figure B-3. Bank Holding Company

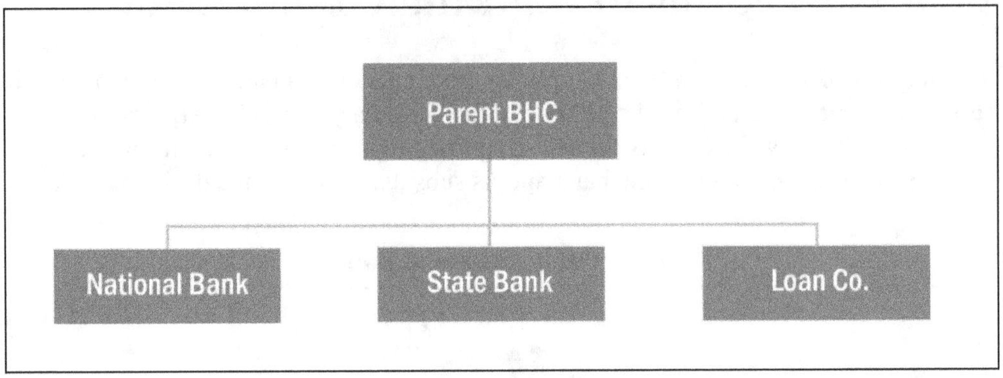

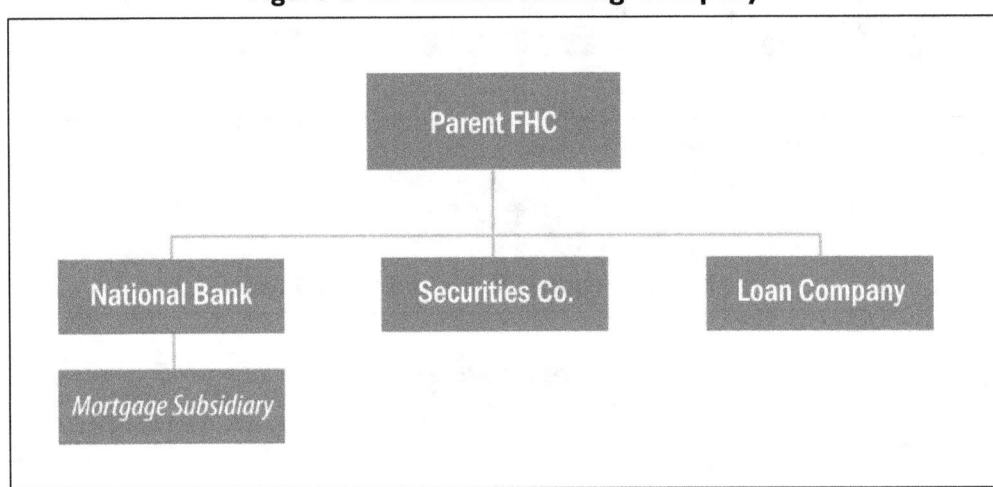

Source: CRS.

Figure B-4. Financial Holding Company

Source: CRS.

Appendix C. Bank Ratings: UFIRS and CAMELS

Federal bank regulators conduct confidential assessments of covered banks. The Federal Financial Institutions Examination Council (FFIEC) helps coordinate the ratings system used by bank examiners so that there is some consistency to the examinations, although the ratings do take into account differences in bank size, sophistication, complexity of activities, and risk profile. The FFIEC adopted the Uniform Financial Institutions Rating System (UFIRS) in 1979. The system was revised in 1996 and is often referred to as the CAMELS rating system. CAMELS stands for Capital adequacy, Asset quality, Management, Earnings, Liquidity, and Sensitivity to market risk. These are measures used to evaluate the safety and soundness of banks. A description of the CAMELS system is found in the Comptrollers Handbook: Bank Supervision Process, provided by the Office of the Comptroller of the Currency (OCC).[43] Market factors can affect more than one category in the CAMELS ratings.

Capital Adequacy

This component assesses the level of capital held by the institution in relation to the risks that it takes. Capital adequacy can be affected by a number of factors, including changes in credit risk, market risk, and the institution's financial condition. Increases in problem assets would require increased capital. Capital adequacy is also supposed to reflect potential risks even if they are technically off of the bank's balance sheet.

Asset Quality

Asset quality refers to existing and potential credit risk associated with a bank's portfolio. Like capital adequacy, this component is supposed to reflect risk even if it is not technically on the bank's balance sheet. Asset quality can include changes in loan default rates, investment performance, exposure to counterparty risk, and all other risks that may affect the value or marketability of an institution's assets.

Management Capability

The governance of the bank, including management and board of directors, is assessed in relation to the nature and scope of the bank's activities. This rating is affected by the level and quality of management oversight. It also includes legal compliance, responsiveness to auditor recommendations, and similar issues.

Earnings Quantity and Quality

The rating of a bank's earnings takes into account current earnings and the sustainability of future earnings. Earnings that rely on favorable tax effects and nonrecurring events receive lower ratings. Similarly, inadequate controls for expenses can reduce the rating for earnings. Difficulties in forecasting and managing risks can also reduce the earnings rating.

---

[43] The Comptrollers handbooks are occasionally updated. The handbook for the Bank Supervision Process can be found at http://www.occ.gov/handbook/banksup.pdf.

Liquidity

Liquidity includes the ability of a bank to meet its expected funding needs. For a given institution size and complexity, this factor assesses the ability of the firm to fulfill its financial obligations in a timely manner. Liquidity refers to the ability to meet short-term funding needs without incurring excessive losses, which might occur if assets had to be sold at a steep discount in a time-pressure situation (or "fire sale"). Liquidity also includes assessments of specific financial categories, such as the trend and stability of deposits, and the expected ability to securitize and sell pools of assets.

Sensitivity to Market Risk

Market risk includes potential changes in the prices of financial assets, such as movements in interest rates, foreign exchange rates, commodity prices, and stock prices. The nature and scope of a bank's activities can affect the markets that it is exposed to; therefore, market risk is closely related to the other CAMELS factors. This rating takes into account management's ability to identify and manage the risks that can arise from the bank's trading activities in financial markets. It also takes into account interest rate risk from nontrading positions, such as any duration mismatch in loans held to maturity.

Appendix D. Regulatory Structure Before the Dodd-Frank Act

Regulatory Agency	Institutions Regulated	Emergency/Systemic Risk Powers	Other Notable Authority
Federal Reserve (The Fed)	Bank holding companies,[a] financial holding companies, state banks that are members of the Federal Reserve System, U.S. branches of foreign banks, foreign branches of U.S. banks	Lender of last resort to member banks (through discount window lending). In "unusual and exigent circumstances" the Fed may lend to *"any individual, partnership, or corporation"*	The Fed issues consumer protection regulations under various federal laws, including the Truth-in-Lending Act
Office of the Comptroller of the Currency (OCC)	National banks, U.S. federal branches of foreign banks		
Federal Deposit Insurance Corporation (FDIC)	Federally insured depository institutions, including state banks that are not members of the Federal Reserve System	After making a determination of systemic risk, the FDIC may invoke broad authority to use the deposit insurance funds to provide an array of assistance to depository institutions	
Office of Thrift Supervision (OTS)	*Federally chartered and insured thrift institutions, savings and loan holding companies*		
National Credit Union Administration (NCUA)	Federally chartered or insured credit unions	Serves as a liquidity lender to credit unions experiencing liquidity shortfalls through the Central Liquidity Facility	Operates a deposit insurance fund for credit unions, the National Credit Union Share Insurance Fund (NCUSIF)
Securities and Exchange Commission (SEC)	Securities exchanges, brokers, and dealers; mutual funds; investment advisers. Registers corporate securities sold to the public	May unilaterally close markets or suspend trading strategies for limited periods	Authorized to set financial accounting standards which all publicly traded firms must use
Commodity Futures Trading Commission (CFTC)	Futures exchanges, brokers, pool operators, advisers	May suspend trading, order liquidation of positions, or raise margins *in emergencies*	
Federal Housing Finance Agency (FHFA)	Fannie Mae, Freddie Mac, and the Federal Home Loan Banks	Acting as conservator (since Sept. 2008) for Fannie and Freddie	

Source: CRS.

Note: Provisions in italics were repealed by Dodd-Frank.

a. See **Appendix B**.

Appendix D: Acronyms

AICPA	American Institute of Certified Public Accountants
BIS	Bank for International Settlements
CAMELS	Capital Adequacy, Asset Quality, Management, Earnings, Liquidity, Sensitivity to Market Risk
CFTC	Commodity Futures Trading Commission
CSE	Consolidated Supervised Entities
DIF	Deposit Insurance Fund
EESA	Emergency Economic Stabilization Act
FASB	Financial Accounting Standards Board
FCM	Futures Commission Merchant
FDIC	Federal Deposit Insurance Corporation
FDICIA	The FDIC Improvement Act of 1991
FFIEC	Federal Financial Institution Examination Council
FHFA	Federal Housing Finance Agency
FHFB	Federal Housing Finance Board
FINRA	Financial Industry Regulatory Authority
FIRREA	The Financial Institutions Reform, Recovery, and Enforcement Act of 1989
FRB	Federal Reserve Board
FSOC	Financial Stability Oversight Council
FSLIC	Federal Savings and Loan Insurance Corporation
FX	Foreign Exchange
GLBA	Gramm-Leach-Bliley Act
GAAP	Generally Accepted Accounting Principles
GSE	Government-Sponsored Enterprise
NCUA	National Credit Union Administration
OCC	Office of the Comptroller of the Currency
OFHEO	Office of Federal Housing Enterprise Oversight
OFR	Office of Financial Research
OTS	Office of Thrift Supervision
PCS	Payment, Clearing, and Settlement Systems
PWG	President's Working Group on Capital Markets
SEC	Securities and Exchange Commission
SIPC	Securities Investor Protection Corporation
SRO	Self Regulatory Organization
UFIRS	Uniform Financial Institutions Rating System

Appendix E. Glossary of Terms

This glossary has been compiled from several earlier CRS reports, the CFTC and SIFMA websites, and other sources.

Affiliate—A corporate relationship of control. Two companies are affiliated when one owns all or a large part of another, or when both are controlled by a third (holding) company. (See "Subsidiary.") All subsidiaries are affiliates, but affiliates that are less than 50% controlled are usually not treated as subsidiaries.

Agency relationship—A business relationship of two parties in which one represents the other in transactions with third parties. The agent negotiates on behalf of the party actually at risk, who is known as the "principal." A commission goes to the agent who does not take on the risk of the transaction; the profit or loss goes to the principal.

Asset-backed security—A bond that represents a share in a pool of debt obligations or other assets. The holder is entitled to some part of the repayment flows from the underlying debt. (See "Securitization.") Mortgage-backed securities and asset backed commercial paper are examples of this.

Bank holding company—A business incorporated under state law, which controls through equity ownership ("holds") one or more banks and, often, other affiliates in financial services as allowed by its regulator, the Federal Reserve. On the federal level, these businesses are regulated through the Bank Holding Company Act.

Bank Holding Company Act—The federal statute under which the Federal Reserve regulates bank holding companies and financial holding companies (FHC). Besides the permissible financial activities enumerated in the Gramm-Leach-Bliley Act (P.L. 106-102), the law provides a mechanism between the Federal Reserve and the Department of the Treasury to decide what is an appropriate new financial activity for FHCs.

Basel Accords—International banking agreements coordinated through the Basel Committee on Bank Supervision (BCBS), which provides recommendations on banking regulations among participating countries.

Blue sky laws—State statutes that govern the offering and selling of securities.

Broker/dealer—An individual or firm that buys and sells securities for itself as well as for customers. Broker/dealers are registered with the Securities and Exchange Commission.

Bubble—Self-reinforcing process in which the price of an asset exceeds its fundamental value for a sustained period, often followed by a rapid price decline. Speculative bubbles are usually associated with a "bandwagon" effect in which speculators rush to buy the commodity (in the case of futures, "to take positions") before the price trend ends, and an even greater rush to sell the commodity (unwind positions) when prices reverse.

Capital requirements—Capital is the owners' stake in an enterprise. It is a critical line of defense when losses occur, both in banking and nonbanking enterprises. Capital requirements help assure that losses that might occur will accrue to the institution incurring them. In the case of banking institutions experiencing problems, capital also serves as a buffer against losses to the federal deposit insurance funds.

Charter conversion—Banking institutions may, with the approval of their regulators, switch their corporate form between: commercial bank or savings institution, National or State charter, and to stockholder ownership from depositor ownership. Various regulatory conditions may encourage switching.

Clearing Organization—An entity through which futures and other derivative transactions are cleared and settled. A clearing organization may be a division or affiliate of a particular exchange, or a freestanding entity. Also called a clearing house, multilateral clearing organization, or clearing association.

Collateralized debt obligation (CDO)—A bond created by the securitization of a pool of asset-backed securities.

Collateralized mortgage obligation (CMO)—A multiclass bond backed by a pool of mortgage pass-through securities or mortgage loans.

Commercial bank—A deposit-taking institution that can make commercial loans, accept checking accounts, and whose deposits are insured by the Federal Deposit Insurance Corporation. National banks are chartered by the Office of the Comptroller of the Currency; state banks, by the individual states.

Commodity Futures Modernization Act of 2000 (CFMA; P.L. 106-554, 114 Stat. 2763)—Overhauled the Commodity Exchange Act to create a flexible structure for the regulation of futures and options trading, and established a broad statutory exemption from regulation for OTC derivatives. Largely repealed by the Dodd-Frank Act.

Community financial institution—As provided for in the Gramm-Leach-Bliley Act, a member of the Federal Home Loan Bank System whose deposits are insured under the Federal Deposit Insurance Act and which has assets of less than $500 million (calculated according to provisions in the law, and in succeeding years to be adjusted for inflation). Such institutions may become members without meeting requirements with regard to the percentage of total assets that must be in residential mortgage loans and may borrow from the Federal Home Loan Banks for small business and agriculture.

Conservatorship—When an insolvent financial institution is reorganized by a regulator with the intent to restoring it to an ongoing business.

Counterparty—The opposite party in a bilateral agreement, contract, or transaction, such as a swap.

Credit Default Swap (CDS)—A tradeable contract in which one party agrees to pay another if a third party experiences a credit event, such as default on a debt obligation, bankruptcy, or credit rating downgrade.

Credit Risk—The risk that a borrower will fail to repay a loan in full, or that a derivatives counterparty will default.

Credit union—A nonprofit financial cooperative of individuals with one or more common bonds (such as employment, labor union membership, or residence in the same neighborhood). May be state or nationally chartered. Credit unions accept deposits of members' savings and transaction balances in the form of share accounts, pay dividends (interest) on them out of earnings, and primarily provide consumer credit to members. The federal regulator for credit unions is the National Credit Union Administration (NCUA).

Dealer—An individual or financial firm engaged in the purchase and sale of securities and commodities such as metals, foreign exchange, etc., for its own account and at its own risk as principal (see broker). Commercial banks are typically limited to acting as dealers in specified high-quality debt obligations, such as those of the federal government.

Depository institution—Customarily refers to commercial banks, savings institutions, and credit unions, since traditionally the greater part of their funding has been in the form of deposits. Deposits are a customer's funds placed with an institution according to agreed-upon terms and conditions and represent a credit to the depositor.

Derivatives—Financial contracts whose value is linked to the price of an underlying commodity or financial variable (such as an interest rate, currency price, or stock index). Ownership of a derivative does not require the holder to actually buy or sell the underlying interest. Derivatives are used by hedgers, who seek to shift risk to others, and speculators, who can profit if they can successfully forecast price trends. Examples include futures contracts, options, and swaps.

Discount window—Figurative term for the Federal Reserve facility for extending credit directly to eligible depository institutions. It may be used to relieve temporary cash shortages at banks and other depository institutions. Borrowers are expected to have tried to borrow elsewhere first and must provide collateral as security for loans. The term derives from the practice whereby bankers would come to a Reserve Bank teller window to obtain credit in the early days of the Federal Reserve System.

Dual banking system—The phrase refers to the fact that banks may be either federally or state-chartered. In the case of state-chartered banks, the state is the primary regulator; for national banks, the Office of the Comptroller of the Currency is the primary regulator.

Electronic fund transfer (EFT) systems—A variety of systems and technologies for transferring funds electronically rather than by paper check.

Exchange—A central marketplace with established rules and regulations where buyers and sellers meet to trade futures and options contracts or securities.

Federal Home Loan Banks—Twelve regional member-owned federally sponsored organizations that extend credit to their member banking institutions, largely to finance mortgages made to homeowners. The 12 FHLBs make up a single government-sponsored enterprise.

Federal safety net—A broad term referring to protection of banking institutions through deposit insurance, discount window credit, other lender of last resort support, and certain forms of regulations to reduce risk. Commercial and industrial companies generally lack any of these cushions against loss.

Financial businesses—In discussions about financial services modernization, usually refers to commercial banks and savings institutions, securities firms, and insurance companies and agents, as contrasted with commercial and industrial firms.

Financial holding company—A form of bank holding company authorized by the Gramm-Leach-Bliley Act that may control one or more banks, securities firms, and insurance companies.

Financial institution—An enterprise that uses its funds chiefly to purchase financial assets such as loans and debt securities, as opposed to tangible property. Financial institutions are differentiated by the manner in which they invest their funds: in loans, bonds, stocks, or some combination; as well as by their sources of funds. Depository financial institutions are differentiated in that they may accept deposits which are federally insured against loss to the depositor. Nondepository financial institutions such as life and property/casualty insurance companies, pension funds, and mutual funds obtain funds through other types of receipts, whose values may fluctuate with market conditions.

Financial subsidiary—Under the Gramm-Leach-Bliley Act, both national and state-chartered banks are authorized to form financial subsidiaries to engage in activities that would not otherwise be permitted within the bank itself, subject to certain limits. Besides the permissible financial activities enumerated in P.L. 106-102, the law provides a mechanism between the U.S. Department of the Treasury and the Federal Reserve to decide what is an appropriate new financial activity for a financial subsidiary.

Firewalls—Barriers to the flow of capital, information, management, and other resources among business units owned by a common entity. In case of financial distress of one operation ("fire"), the "walls" are intended to prevent the spread of loss to the other units—especially to banking units. Example: losses in a securities subsidiary of a holding company could not be covered by any of the holding company's bank subsidiaries.

Foreign bank—Banks and their holding companies headquartered in other countries may have a variety of financial operations in the United States: U.S.-chartered subsidiary banks, agencies, branches, and representative offices. Their primary federal regulator is the Federal Reserve, under the International Banking Act of 1978 as amended. States and the Office of the Comptroller of the Currency may also regulate them, depending on whether they have a state or federal charter.

Forward Contract—A cash transaction in which a buyer and seller agree upon delivery of a specified quality and quantity of goods at a specified future date.

Functional regulation—Regulatory arrangements based on activity ("function") rather than organizational structure. The Gramm-Leach-Bliley Act called for more functional regulation than in the past.

Futures Contract—An agreement to purchase or sell a commodity for delivery in the future: (1) at a price that is determined at initiation of the contract; (2) that obligates each party to the contract to fulfill the contract at the specified price; (3) that is used to assume or shift price risk; and (4) that may be satisfied by delivery or offset.

Glass-Steagall Act—Part of the Banking Act of 1933; divided the commercial and investment banking industries. The Gramm-Leach-Bliley Act repealed two sections of the act dealing with the relationship between banks and securities firms.

Government-sponsored enterprise (GSE)—GSEs are private companies with government charters. Government sponsorship typically gives them a funding advantage over purely private competitors, while their charters restrict the kinds of businesses they may conduct.

Gramm-Leach-Bliley Act of 1999—P.L. 106-102, also known as the Financial Services Modernization Act, authorized increased affiliations between banks, securities firms, and insurers. Permitted the establishment of financial holding companies, under the regulation of the Federal Reserve. Also addressed privacy protection for consumers' financial data.

Haircut—In computing the value of assets for purposes of capital, segregation, or margin requirements, a percentage reduction from the stated value (e.g., book value or market value) to account for possible declines in value that may occur before assets can be liquidated.

Hedge funds—Hedge funds are essentially unregulated mutual funds. They are pools of invested money that buy and sell stocks and bonds and many other assets, including precious metals, commodities, foreign currencies, and derivatives (contracts whose prices are derived from those of other financial instruments). Hedge funds are limited to qualified investors with high net worth.

Hedging—Investing with the intention of reducing the impact of adverse movements in interest rates, commodities, or securities prices. Typically, the hedging instrument gains value as the hedged item loses value, and vice versa.

Insolvent—A firm whose liabilities exceed its assets.

Institutional regulation—Regulation that is institution-specific as contrasted with activity-specific (see functional regulation).

Investment bank—A financial intermediary, active in the securities business. Investment banking functions include underwriting (marketing newly registered securities to individual or institutional investors), counseling regarding merger and acquisition proposals, brokerage services, advice on corporate financing, and proprietary trading.

Investment bank holding company—A holding company for securities firms authorized under the Gramm-Leach-Bliley Act. Such holding companies are subject to regulation by the Securities and Exchange Commission.

Issuer—A person or entity (including a company or bank) that offers securities for sale. The issuing of securities, where the proceeds accrue to the issuer, is distinct from the secondary, or resale, market, where securities are traded among investors.

Lender of last resort—Governmental lender that acts as the ultimate source of credit in the financial system. In the United States, the Federal Reserve has this role.

Leverage—In derivatives markets, leverage (or "gearing") often refers to the ability to control large dollar amounts of a commodity or security with a comparatively small amount of capital. In banking, the term leverage is often used to describe the amount of a bank's assets that are funded with debt rather than equity. In banking, leverage is typically the ratio of lending to equity.

Limited-purpose bank—Although generally commercial firms may not conduct a banking business, some exceptions exist. Examples: Nonbank banks are banks that either accept deposits or make commercial loans but cannot do both. Such banks grew up through a loophole in the law, which was closed by the Competitive Equality Banking Act of 1987 (CEBA). Credit card banks conduct credit card operations. Industrial loan companies in a few states may offer restricted banking services.

Liquidity—The ability to trade an asset quickly without significantly affecting its price, or the condition of a market with many buyers and sellers present. Also, the ability of a person or firm to access credit markets.

Liquidity risk—The possibility that the market for normally-liquid assets will suddenly dry up, leaving firms unable to convert assets into cash. Also, the risk that other firms will refuse to extend credit on any terms to a firm that is perceived as distressed.

Market risk—The risk that the price of a tradeable security or asset will decline, resulting in a loss to the holder.

Merchant banker—A European style investment banker concentrating on corporate deals, in which it may invest its own funds.

Money market mutual fund (MMF)—A form of mutual fund that pools funds of individuals and other investors for investment in high-grade, short-term debt and bank deposits paying market rates of return. Examples of these money market instruments include U.S. Treasury bills, certificates of deposit, and commercial paper. In addition to the investment features, most MMFs offer check-writing redemption features.

Moral hazard—The tendency of people to take more risks once another party has agreed to provide protection. Regulatory interventions to bail out failing firms are often said to create moral hazard, on the assumption that others will expect to be saved from their mistakes, too.

Mortgage-backed security (MBS)—A bond backed by a pool of mortgage loans. The bondholders receive a share of the interest and principal payments on the underlying mortgages. The cash flows may be divided among different classes of bonds, called tranches.

Mutual fund—An investing company that pools the funds of individuals and other investors, and uses them to purchase large amounts of debt or equity obligations of businesses and sometimes debt obligations of governments. The owners of the mutual fund hold proportional shares in the entire pool of securities in which a fund invests. Owners pay taxes on their distributions from a fund; the mutual fund itself is not normally subject to federal or state income taxation.

Naked option—The sale of a call or put option without holding an equal and opposite position in the underlying instrument.

Operational risk—The possibility that a financial institution will suffer losses from a failure to process transactions properly, from accounting mistakes, from rogue traders or other forms of insider fraud, or from other causes arising inside the institution.

Over-the-counter (OTC)—Trading that does not occur on a centralized exchange or trading facility. OTC transactions can occur electronically or over the telephone.

Ponzi Scheme—Named after Charles Ponzi, a man with a remarkable criminal career in the early 20th century, the term has been used to describe pyramid arrangements whereby an enterprise makes payments to investors from the proceeds of a later investment rather than from profits of the underlying business venture, as the investors expected, and gives investors the impression that a legitimate profit-making business or investment opportunity exists, where in fact it is a mere fiction.

Prompt corrective action (PCA)—A framework of bank regulation in which banks with insufficient capital must undertake remedial action to improve their capital positions. In the United States, the PCA framework has five categories of bank capitalization. Financially troubled banks are required to take prompt action as directed by the relevant agencies to remedy identified deficiencies.

Receivership—When an insolvent financial institution is taken over with the intent to liquidate its assets.

Regulatory Arbitrage—If different contract types or firm charters can be used to achieve similar ends, but have different regulatory treatment, then regulatory arbitrage refers to attempts to receive the least burdensome regulatory treatment for a given activity. In economics, arbitrage is the practice of taking advantage of a price difference between two or more markets.

Resolution Trust Corporation (RTC)—The agency set up to resolve savings and loans declared failed beginning in 1989. Between 1989 and mid-1995, the Resolution Trust Corporation closed or otherwise resolved 747 thrifts with total assets of $394 billion.

Repurchase Agreement (Repo)—A contract in which one party sells a contract (typically a bond or other debt contract) to buyer, with a commitment to repurchase the contract on a future date at a specified price. In economics, repurchase agreements have similar characteristics to collateralized lending.

Savings association—A savings and loan association, mutual savings bank, or federal savings bank, whose primary function has traditionally been to encourage personal saving (thrift) and home buying through mortgage lending. In recent years, such institutions' charters have been expanded to allow them to provide commercial loans and a broader range of consumer financial services. The federal regulator for most savings associations is the Office of Thrift Supervision. Also known as savings and loans, thrifts, and mutual savings banks.

Securities Investor Protection Corporation (SIPC)—A private nonprofit membership corporation set up under federal law to provide financial protection for the customers of failed brokers and/or dealers. SIPC is a liquidator; it has no supervisory or regulatory responsibilities for its members, nor is it authorized to bail out or in other ways assist a failing firm.

Securitization—The process of transforming a cash flow, typically from debt repayments, into a new marketable security. Holders of the securitized instrument receive interest and principal payments as the underlying loans are repaid. Types of loans that are frequently securitized are home mortgages, credit card receivables, student loans, small business loans, and car loans.

Self-regulatory organizations (SROs)—National securities or futures exchanges, national securities or futures associations, clearing agencies and the Municipal Securities Rulemaking Board are all authorized to make and enforce rules governing market participants. The respective federal regulatory agency has authority in connection with SROs and may require them to adopt or modify their rules. Examples of SROs in the securities industry include the Financial Industry Regulatory Authority (FINRA), and the New York Stock Exchange.

Shadow banking—The funding of loans through firms that do not have bank charters, through securities markets, or the funding of banks with sources other than deposits. Often, the term shadow banking is used to describe financial intermediation with at least one deviation from a model in which banks raise all of their funds from sources with government guarantees (such as deposit insurance) and banks have access to emergency government lending facilities, such as the Federal Reserve's discount window.

Special-purpose entities (SPEs)—Also referred to as off–balance-sheet arrangements, SPEs are legal entities created to perform a specific financial function or transaction. They isolate financial risk from the sponsoring institution and provide less-expensive financing. The assets, liabilities, and cash flows of an SPE do not appear on the sponsoring institution's books.

Speculation—A venture or undertaking of an enterprising nature, especially one involving considerable financial risk on the chance of unusual profit.

State regulation—Under the dual system of bank regulation, states as well as the federal government may charter, regulate, and supervise depository institutions. States are the primary regulators in the insurance field. States also have authority over securities companies, mortgage lending companies, personal finance companies, and other types of companies offering financial services.

Structured debt—Debt that has been customized for the buyer, often by incorporating complex derivatives.

Subordinated debt—Debt over which senior debt takes priority. In the event of bankruptcy, subordinated debt holders receive payment only after senior debt claims are paid in full.

Subsidiary—A company whose controlling shares are owned 50% or more by another ("parent") corporation. Like companies with less than 50% ownership, it is an affiliate of the controlling company. A subsidiary is usually consolidated for regulatory and reporting purposes with its parent.

Swap—The exchange of one asset or liability for a similar asset or liability for the purpose of lengthening or shortening maturities, or otherwise shifting risks. For example, parties could exchange a fixed interest rate stream of income for a floating rate stream of income, or a stream of income based on one currency's exchange rate for a stream of income based on another currency's exchange rate.

Systemic Risk—The term *systemic risk* does not have a single, agreed-upon definition. Some define systemic risk as the risk an institution faces that it cannot diversify against. In other circumstances, systemic risk is defined as the risk that the linkages between institutions may affect the financial system as a whole, through a dynamic sometimes referred to as contagion.

Thrift holding company—Also known as a savings and loan holding company, a business that controls one or more savings associations. These holding companies are regulated under the Home Owners' Loan Act by the Office of Thrift Supervision.

Too-big-to-fail doctrine—An implicit regulatory policy holding that very large financial institutions must be rescued by the government, because their failure would destabilize the entire financial system. (See "Moral Hazard.")

Umbrella supervision—The term applied to comprehensive regulation of a holding company and its parts by one or more holding company regulator(s).

Underwriter—For securities markets, see investment bankers. For insurance, underwriters are the life, health and property-casualty companies that receive premiums and pay off losses and other risks as they occur. The underwriters bear the risks of losses and expenses exceeding receipts.

Unitary thrift holding company (UTHC)—A holding company that owns a single thrift institution. A distinction between UTHCs and other thrift holding companies has been that a UTHC could be involved in any lines of business, whereas the others have been restricted to certain activities primarily financial in nature. The Gramm-Leach-Bliley Act limits the commercial activities and affiliations of new UTHCs.

Universal bank—An organizational model typical of some foreign countries whereby a bank can exist as an operating enterprise and own directly a variety of other businesses. (See "Subsidiary.") It contrasts with the banking model typical in the United States where the parent holding company owns several different businesses, all structurally separate. (See "Affiliate.") In practice, the two approaches are not exclusive.

Volcker Rule—Section 619 of the Dodd-Frank Act, which prohibits insured depository banks and their affiliated firms from engaging in proprietary trading or affiliating with hedge funds.

Author Contact Information

Edward V. Murphy
Specialist in Financial Economics
tmurphy@crs.loc.gov, 7-6201

Acknowledgments

The author gratefully acknowledges substantial prior work by Mark Jickling and Walter Eubanks, and helpful comments from CRS colleagues, especially, Marc Labonte and Maureen Murphy.

www.ingramcontent.com/pod-product-compliance
Lightning Source LLC
Chambersburg PA
CBHW081617170526
45166CB00009B/3010